ALTAR WORK 101

A SIMPLE GUIDE TO SUCCESSFUL MINISTRY
IN THE SPIRIT-FILLED CHURCH

Rodne

Harrison House
Tulsa, Oklahoma

Unless otherwise indicated, all Scripture quotations are taken from the *King James Version* of the Bible.

Altar Work 101: A Simple Guide to
Successful Ministry in the Spirit-filled Church
ISBN 1-57794-015-6
Copyright © 1998 by Rodney Lynch
P. O. Box 3315
Broken Arrow, Oklahoma 74013-3315

Published by Harrison House, Inc.
P. O. Box 35035
Tulsa, Oklahoma 74153

Dedication

This work is dedicated to my pastor, Willie George. I am grateful to God for giving me the privilege to have worked for and with Pastor George.

Special thanks:

...to Rev. Buddy Bell, who encouraged me to write this.

...to Steve and Leanna Willis and to Wendy Curlis. Thank you for your help.

Contents

Introduction: To the Worker   7

To the Leadership   7

1   "Why Should I Be an Altar Worker?"   9

2   Training Tips...and More   23

3   Guidelines for Altar Workers   33

4   Ministry in the Prayer Room: The Specifics   49

5   Follow-up Is Essential   69

6   Scheduling Your Workers   73

7   Altar Work and the Law   81

8   Sample Forms and Handouts   91

Introduction
•••

To the Worker:

Now more than ever, it's time we be about our Father's business. I sincerely hope the information shared in this book will encourage you to become involved in this important part of the ministry of Jesus. I trust it will help you to excel at altar working.

The best way to excel at any ministry you are involved in is to love the people. Let that be your *vision*, then the *discipline* you need to learn the program and to study the guidelines will be there. God will also provide the *boldness* you need to share the truth of God's Word with those who are seeking to know it.

> **And whatsoever ye do, do it heartily, as to the Lord, and not unto men;**
>
> **Knowing that of the Lord ye shall receive the reward of the inheritance: for ye serve the Lord Christ.**
>
> **Colossians 3:23,24**

To the Leadership:

Because of the complexities of leadership and the sensitive nature of today's laws, we need now more than ever to be sure we have excellence of ministry in every area of church function.

The purpose of this book is to share with you an instrumental plan for altar working, regardless of your church's size. I want to prepare you to handle in an organized fashion the responses to the altar calls in your services, but most importantly, to help you meet the needs of those who respond, whether small or large in number.

Each church is different, having in a sense a personality or character of its own. I believe this material can be used to get your program running smoothly so that you as pastor can, for the most part, be free of concern about what is happening in your prayer room. Use it as a starting place, then add your own ideas to fit the needs of your church.

"Why Should I Be an Altar Worker?"
• • •

Let's lay a foundation for involvement in what Ephesians 4:12 calls **the work of the ministry.** God has a specific call on every believer's life. He has given each of us the privilege of being involved in the most important work in the world: the spreading of the Gospel of Jesus Christ.

BE WHAT GOD WANTS YOU TO BE
• • •

There is a specific call on you to be whatever you know God wants you to be. Of course, not every believer is called into some sort of pulpit ministry. God has led people in various directions. For instance, He has called some people to enter into politics and other people to be in law enforcement. (Romans 13:1-7.)

If you are not called into the fivefold ministry, perhaps you are wondering specifically what God wants you to do. He will allow you to make a choice. You can know what God wants you to do by following your heart. Psalm 37:4 says if you delight yourself in the Lord, He will give you the desires of your heart. (Author's paraphrase.)

Follow after whatever you are drawn to as a career, what you feel you would enjoy doing. Of course, you don't want to become involved in anything that goes contrary to sound doctrine. For instance, God would never call people to go out and rob banks in order to have money that they could then give to Him.

You can fulfill God's specific will for your life — whether it is as a doctor, housekeeper, chef, sanitation engineer or any other occupation — as long as you are a doer of God's Word while involved in your profession.

GENERAL CALLINGS ON ALL OF US
. . .

There are some general callings we all have for which we are accountable.

First, we all — every one of us — are called to know God and to obey Him. This was known even in Old Testament times.

> **Let us hear the conclusion of the whole matter: Fear God, and keep his commandments: for this is the whole *duty* of man.**
> **For God shall bring every work into judgment, with every secret thing, whether it be good, or whether it be evil.**
>
> **Ecclesiastes 12:13,14**

God has called, and is calling, *every* human being into a relationship with Him. If we were to remove the italicized word *duty* from the last half of verse 13, it would read this way: "for this is the whole of man." Remember, to fear God and to obey Him is the first calling you have on your life.

You are to know your Creator intimately. That calling from God will never change.

This leaves us constantly challenged to maintain that intimacy with God through the reading and meditation of God's Word, along with prayer, worship and obedience to Him. There is nothing boring about Christianity. Remember, I am talking here about God's callings, not His commandments. A calling is an option given you to obey God. A commandment is just that — a commandment, not a request.

The second calling is that of sharing Jesus in words and actions.

> **Therefore if any man be in Christ, he is a new creature: old things are passed away; behold, all things are become new.**
>
> **And all things are of God, who hath reconciled us to himself by Jesus Christ, and hath given to us the ministry of reconciliation;**
>
> **To wit, that God was in Christ, reconciling the world unto himself, not imputing their trespasses unto them; and hath committed unto us the word of reconciliation.**
>
> **Now then we are ambassadors for Christ, as though God did beseech you by us: we pray you in Christ's stead, be ye reconciled to God.**
>
> **2 Corinthians 5:17-20**

You may be a doctor, a salesman or in some other profession. But remember: first of all, you are a child of God and are called as an ambassador for Christ. No matter what your profession may be here on earth, it will pass away. In heaven, there won't be any need for physicians, plumbers and insurance salesmen.

So don't fail to recognize your call to be an ambassador for Christ.

The final call is to be doing the work of the ministry in your local church. Look at Ephesians 4:11-16:

> And he gave some, apostles; and some, prophets; and some, evangelists; and some, pastors and teachers;
>
> For the perfecting [maturing] of the saints, for the work of the ministry, for the edifying of the body of Christ:
>
> Till we all come in the unity of the faith, and of the knowledge of the Son of God, unto a perfect man, unto the measure of the stature of the fulness of Christ:
>
> That we henceforth be no more children, tossed to and fro, and carried about with every wind of doctrine, by the sleight of men, and cunning craftiness, whereby they lie in wait to deceive;
>
> But speaking the truth in love, may grow up into him in all things, which is the head, even Christ:
>
> From whom the whole body fitly joined together and compacted by that which every joint supplieth, according to the effectual working in the measure of every part, maketh increase of the body unto the edifying of itself in love.

The fivefold ministry gifts are gifts of *service*. People in these positions are called to help us in the Body of Christ to grow into a place of maturity and to prepare us to work in the ministry.

Another translation of verse 12 reads this way: **in order to get His holy people ready to serve as workers.**[1]

But if we are not called to be an apostle, prophet, evangelist, pastor or teacher, then what ministry are we to fulfill — the ministry of an ambassador for Christ?

Yes. But there is another most important ministry gift pointed out in Scripture: the ministry of helps.

THE MINISTRY OF HELPS
...

Now ye are the body of Christ, and members in particular.

And God hath set some in the church, first apostles, secondarily prophets, thirdly teachers, after that miracles, then gifts of healings, helps, governments, diversities of tongues.

1 Corinthians 12:27,28

Notice the word *helps* in verse 28. Scripture is telling us God set the ministry of helps into the Church. This is a part of the calling God places on the life of *every* believer: that we each are to be involved in our local church in some capacity. The helps ministry is one area of church service.

That is why every church member should be involved in some way at their church, whether as altar worker, nursery worker or parking-lot attendant. Let's look again at Ephesians 4:16:

---

[1] William F. Beck. *The New Testament in the Language of Today.* (St. Louis: Concordia, 1963).

> From whom the whole body fitly joined
> together and compacted by that which every joint
> supplieth, according to the effectual working in
> the measure of every part, maketh increase of the
> body unto the edifying of itself in love.

Notice that *every* member of the Body of Christ is important for "making increase of the Body." Imagine what it would be like if the Body of Christ — the *whole* Body — were to get involved in the work of the ministry. The helps ministry is a viable, God-ordained ministry to which we all are called.

The fivefold ministry serves the Church. Even the gift of the evangelist has been given to the Church. We all can't win everyone. Some people just won't receive what God is saying through us. But when God sends an evangelist into our midst, there is someone we can bring the lost to hear, since God has given the evangelist a special anointing to win the lost.

So the evangelist is a tool, a gift from the Lord, who can be used by the believer to augment his/her personal ministry as an ambassador for Christ. It is, however, your responsibility as a believer to go out to the lost and to compel them to come to the services or meetings to hear the evangelist preach. It is also *your* responsibility to "make increase of the Body" by being a servant.

> But it shall not be so among you: but
> whosoever will be great among you, let him be
> your minister;
> And whosoever will be chief among you, let
> him be your servant:

> Even as the Son of man came not to be minis-
> tered unto, but to minister, and to give his life a
> ransom for many.

Matthew 20:26-28

Another translation renders the last half of verse 27 as: **must be the willing slave of all.**[2] Then the last half of verse 28 in yet another translation reads: **not to be waited on, but to wait on other people.**[3]

We all are called to this service of helps so that the local church can thrive. It will then grow as a place of benefit for us in our own relationship with the Lord (**for the perfecting of the saints** — Ephesians 4:12) and as a place for us to bring the lost. If we think of it as such and use it this way, the local church should be a tool for our benefit, like the evangelists, to aid us in fulfilling our call of being ambassadors for Christ.

WHY BE AN ALTAR WORKER?
...

Why specifically should a person be an altar worker?

It Brings Great Joy

The beauty of altar working is to be personally involved in seeing the lost come to Christ and in seeing them be filled with the Holy Spirit.

---

[2] *The New English Bible.* (New York, New York: Oxford University Press and Cambridge University Press, 1961).

[3] Edgar J. Goodspeed. *The New Testament: An American Translation.* (Chicago: University of Chicago Press, 1923, 1948).

An altar worker would also be able to share in the joy of seeing prodigal sons and daughters come home. Even if you personally didn't "reel in the net" as an altar worker you would be the first believer to have contact with these people in this wonderful time in their lives.

As I have said, there is nothing more wonderful than being involved in some capacity in an individual's conversion or repentance experience. There is great joy in this!

It Is Valuable Training Ground

Remember, we all are called to be ambassadors for Christ. What better way would there be for you to prepare, apart from your own personal time with God, than to be taught how to lead someone to Jesus or be involved in the restoration of a person's fellowship with God.

And how many believers do you know who have the confidence to lead someone in prayer to receive the baptism in the Holy Spirit? This work is wonderful training ground.

If you have studied and trained to help those who respond to an altar call at your church, think how much confidence that can build in you to share with others *outside* your church. Speaking publicly for some can be scary.

Many years ago *McCall's Magazine* published the results of a survey in which it polled a number of people regarding their fears. The number-one fear on the list of ten was not death, as you may have thought. I was surprised to learn it was the fear of public speaking.

Being an altar worker can help you get out of your comfort zone — which you need to do! And so does everyone else!

This is not to say it will be easy; but as you get through those first few times of sharing with another person, I believe you will find your confidence being built up. Combine the proper training with a little experience, along with some prayer for boldness (Acts 4:29,30), and you will have phenomenal potential as an ambassador for Christ. Most believers don't. So be different!

Altar workers take on a *serious* responsibility in their task, but it has tremendous rewards. If you are a people person, this kind of work should be right for you. But even if you aren't a people person, it can be right for you, too! You probably need to loosen up a bit and get out of your comfort zone.

I am not saying that being an altar worker is for everybody, but it has benefits that would be a blessing to anyone who "put it on" for a while. That's a good way to find your niche if you aren't certain what to do in the helps ministry. Try out different areas until one fits well, feels good, and you enjoy serving in that ministry. It takes the *whole* Body to make the increase, so do your part.

It Fulfills God's Plan

Lastly, you should be an altar worker, or in the helps ministry somewhere, because *the happiest people in the Church are the ones who are involved.*

Generally, we humans value most what we invest in. If you will invest in what your local church is doing by becoming involved — by doing the work of God — it will cause you to value your local church more because you are a part of fulfilling God's plan for that church. You are helping your pastor bring to pass the vision God has given him for your church. In a sense it's your vision too, because *the church staff can't do it all!*

So, let's *all* get to work and hasten the return of the Lord.

RECRUITING WORKERS
...

To the church leadership I would say, God wants to bless your church! He wants it to grow. He wants you to have a new building if you need it or to fill up the one you now have. He wants to fill your altar with the lost who are seeking salvation and the baptism in the Holy Spirit, or with those who have backslidden and wish to restore their fellowship with God.

Is that happening in your church? Are you pleased with how your church is growing? To answer these questions you must look within yourself. If the answer to either is no, you need to consider the following questions as a part of your search for an answer:

- Would you be prepared for the growth if it came?

- Could you handle a large crowd of twenty or more people responding all at once to an altar call?

- Would they all be *effectively* ministered to, then followed up on?

My premise is this: God will give you what you are ready for!

Make a Plan

When it comes to new converts, you might want to think of your local church as a big orphanage. God isn't going to send an overwhelming bunch of new babies to an orphanage (church) that wouldn't be able to take care of them. Those little ones could die without proper attention.

So what do you need to do?

Get ready — that's what!

Make a plan for church growth and be sure you have enough good workers trained to carry it out. Then you will be ready for the babies (new converts) to come.

Apply this to *every* aspect of your church and see if the Lord doesn't bring to light some different areas that need attention.

Make sure you are ready to minister effectively to those who respond to your altar calls. Whether the number is large or small, this is serious business. God has given us the privilege and responsibility of being His co-workers. We mustn't allow the term *"excellence in ministry"* to become just a cliché.

Go Fishing!

Recruiting in some ways is like fishing. When you go fishing, you have a purpose, whether it is to provide some food or just to get in some relaxation. A need is being met when fish are caught.

This applies to recruiting workers in your church. You have a *need*: there are blank spots in your altar workers' schedule (or any other area of helps ministry). You need to catch some "fish," or workers, so you go where those "fish" hang out — your church.

You, as their pastor or leader, have to become the *hook, line and sinker!* You must tell the people about your need on a regular basis, because there will always be change in any growing church, with people coming and going.

The *bait* you use is simple: tell them God's rewards for faithful, diligent workers. You must "put them in remembrance." Make the bait as attractive as you can. God expects us to be conscious of the reward! (Hebrews 11:6; 1 Corinthians 3:13,14; 2 Corinthians 5:10; 2 Timothy 6:7,8; Revelation 2:7,11,17,26; 3:5,12,21.)

Getting your people involved in the helps ministry is one of *your* responsibilities as pastor or leader.

> **And he gave some, apostles; and some, prophets; and some, evangelists; and some, pastors and teachers;**
>
> **For the perfecting [maturing] of the saints, for the work of the ministry, for the edifying of the body of Christ.**
>
> **Ephesians 4:11,12**

Although involvement in your church's helps ministry in no way completely fulfills the call of God to ministry in each believer's life (see 2 Corinthians 5:18-20), it is up to you as the leader to provide places of service within your local church setting.

When you ask people to work in the helps ministry, keep in mind that you are doing *them* a service. You are not just using them for what they can do for you. Rather, you are providing a means for growth in their character as they learn to serve, as well as opening another channel of blessing for God to work through their lives. Think in terms of *mutual benefit*.

BE SELECTIVE!
...

It is so important for church leaders to be selective of whom they choose to be altar workers.

> **And we beseech you, brethren, to know them which labour among you....**
>
> **1 Thessalonians 5:12**

To beseech means to request as a favor. The favor requested here by the apostle Paul is more for our (leadership's) benefit than for his. Godly wisdom is to be used by church leaders to check out those who are working for them. This applies to every area of helps ministry, but especially to altar workers and to people involved in the children's department.

I highly recommend police checks of your workers. You should request pastoral references and personal references, particularly for children's workers.

If you are in a small church with few workers, please *do not* allow your need to cause you to compromise integrity, either of yourself or of your church. With Plan B (explained in chapter 3), if necessity arose, you could handle any number of respondents with only a couple of altar workers in the prayer room. So, like Paul said in Scripture, I beseech you, do yourself a favor and "know those who labor among you."

The training procedures discussed later in this book should help you communicate what you expect from your workers and will provide you with some insight into their character.

REFERENCES

...

Is this important? Absolutely! References are scripturally required (1 Timothy 3:7); and of course, once checked, they can provide additional valuable insight into a person's character.

Here are some questions you might ask of the people listed as references:

1. How long have you known this person?

2. What was your relationship with him/her?

3. Was he/she faithful in church attendance?

4. Would you consider this person to be a stable and committed believer?

5. In your opinion, does he/she have any negative traits?

6. What are his/her strong points?

Remember: all answers you receive should be held in confidence!

Training Tips...and More
•••

Training is *essential* in every area of the helps ministry. Altar workers should have the confidence of knowing they are well equipped and properly trained to do their job. Yes, there will be work involved in being an altar worker. Studying and memorizing takes effort. But remember this: people value more highly what they have invested in than what comes for free.

The person in charge of the altar workers should be chosen by the pastor and given the responsibility of training them. This will establish rapport and respect. I would, however, encourage the pastor to occasionally speak to the workers.

Good constant communication is one of the cornerstones of all relationships. Maintaining communication should be a priority between the leaders and the workers. I have found that meetings are the most convenient way for them to communicate with each other.

There needs to be a balance in this area, however. Having too many meetings can cause problems, for example, by placing too great a demand on the workers' free time. On the other hand, not enough meetings can be detrimental to the effectiveness of the program. Things will not be done correctly when there is a lack of training. So regular training sessions are an absolute necessity, only in moderation; don't have meetings every week.

Since communication with all the workers will never cease to be a necessity, the leader needs to be flexible in scheduling these meetings. If you have a steady influx of new workers, have meetings more often. Only the trainees need to attend one or two of them. The experienced workers will be able to find out what is going on at "Before Service Meetings," which will be discussed later in this chapter.

Here is a guideline for a training session:

ALTAR WORKER TRAINING SESSION OUTLINE
. . .

I. Before the session

    A. Advertise it. Recruit with these meetings. Turn your workers into recruiters. Have them invite church members whom they think would make good altar workers.

    B. Have an abundance of materials, such as Guidelines and Altar Worker Availability Reports (to be discussed later in the book). It's better to have something you don't need than to need something you don't have.

    C. Know your material!

II. The meeting

    A. Start on time!

    B. Distribute materials, such as Helps Ministry Applications and Guidelines. Share from your heart 1 Corinthians 12:28. Helps is a ministry! Most believers are called to helps — not to be apostles, prophets, evangelists, pastors and teachers. (Ephesians 4:11,12.) God did not set up the Church with too many leaders and not enough servants.

C. Go over the Guidelines word for word. This will take most of your time.

D. Breaks may be needed, so allow for them. *The mind can only receive what the seat can endure.*

E. Take questions after you have finished going over the Guidelines.

F. Allot yourself a minimum of ninety minutes for the meeting.

G. Be prepared to answer their questions.

H. Go over the books that will be given to respondents. (You should know what's in them!) Give the workers a brief synopsis or let them take a copy home, read it and return it.

III. Go over scheduling procedures and show a sample schedule.

IV. Clean up loose ends.

V. Have some fellowship with snacks.

GIVE THEM A TEST...OR TWO
...

Written Test

Because of the need for excellence in the area of altar working, I recommend that before any person is allowed to work in the prayer room as an altar worker, he or she be given a written test on the procedures laid out in that church's guidelines. This will help both leaders and workers to know how familiar they are with the program. It also will give leaders a basis for making the decision as to when people will be allowed to start as altar workers.

The test does not need to be extremely long; twenty or twenty-five questions would be sufficient. These questions should not be too easy, however; and each one needs to make a point.

Leaders may, of course, compose the test with whatever types of questions they choose, i.e., true or false, multiple choice, essay, fill in the blank. I like to mix them up.

Oral Test

I also suggest that each new worker go through the three areas of ministry orally with the service leader or captain. This will be a means of further assuring both leaders and workers that they are ready to go on to the next step.

Regarding the oral test, the leader must strive for a flow in the worker's message to respondents. The test examiner should check to see that the church's recommended Scriptures are being used by the workers in each of the three areas: salvation, restoration and the baptism in the Holy Spirit. Workers should not give a word-for-word recitation of a script unless they are required by leadership to memorize it.

SAMPLE TEST QUESTIONS

Fill in the Blank:

1. I must meet in the prayer room _____ minutes before the service I am working.

   Answer: 20

2. Our purpose in providing this ministry is to
_____ those people responding to an altar call
that they have received from the Lord what they came for.

Answer: assure

Essay:

3. An altar worker's sharing should be confined to what areas and why?

4. Briefly write out your procedures once you are in the prayer room under Plan A.

True or False:

5. You should respond and come forward immediately when the pastor calls you. True or false?

Answer: False

6. Be sure to give everyone the following: *The New Birth, In Him, Why Tongues?, Redeemed*. True or false?

Answer: False

Multiple Choice:

7. Which of the following is correct concerning Follow-up Reports:

   A. They must be filled out completely.

   B. Sign your name and the date in the appropriate places.

   C. Fill in the "Remarks" section.

   D. Take the white copy of the report home with you and bring it to the following service.

   E. All of the above.

Answer: E

8. Using Plan B, which of the following is correct?

   A. As much as possible, altar workers (AW) should be seated with respondents (R) as follows: AW, R, R, AW, R, R, AW

   B. One person will lead the people most of the time while in the prayer room.

   C. Find one person and help him/her with the material. Then you may leave.

   Answer: B

Combination:

9. I have _____ hours to make contact with the person I have helped.

   Answer: 48

10. I should take _____ minutes — and no more! — to complete my time with the respondent.

   Answer: 10 to 20

11. List all the materials you are to give the respondent for restoration:

   Answers: *In Him, Redeemed,* "Your Next Steps"

12. What two items should you expect to find on the monthly schedule?

   Answers: Your schedule; important announcements

13. After entering the prayer room, you should first get your materials so that you may have them ready to give away. True or false?

   Answer: False

14. The only subjects you are to discuss with any respondents are salvation, restoration and the baptism in the Holy Spirit. True or false?

Answer: True

15. Which of these Scriptures should not be included in your sharing about salvation?

    A. Romans 10:9,10

    B. John 1:12

    C. John 3:23

    D. 1 John 5:13

    Answer: John 1:12

16. Which of these Scriptures does not pertain to the baptism in the Holy Spirit, relative to our purpose?

    A. Acts 2:4

    B. Mark 16:15

    C. Acts 2:38,39

    D. Acts 1:4-8

    Answer: Mark 16:15

17. When Plan B is being used, the service captain will release the altar workers to _____ _____ on those receiving the _____.

    Answers: lay hands; baptism in the Holy Spirit

18. I must attend _____ _____ _____ only when I am scheduled to work.

    Answer: Before Service Meetings

19. Write out briefly what you are to do when Plan B is in effect *after* you have prayed with candidates for the baptism in the Holy Spirit.

Answers: Help respondents to fill out a Follow-up Report; wait in prayer room or designated area to get forms to follow up on.

20. Why are you an altar worker?

Important: You can use these tests to help you know those who are laboring among you. Be sure some of your test questions are worded in such a way that you will be able to detect any tendencies to go beyond the guidelines of your program (see question 3).

LEADERSHIP OPTIONS

...

To the leader in charge of finding altar workers, I would say: choose carefully! It's easier to give authority than to take it away.

Depending on the size of your church or your workload, you may want to give some of your best altar workers a chance to lead. You may choose to call them service leaders or captains. It's important that you show proper support for these leaders. Let them know they would be working with you in an "associate" or "assistant" leadership capacity (not necessarily pastoral) and would be required to take on the following responsibilities:

1. Be in charge of the intercessory prayer meeting for altar workers prior to the service. (See section entitled, "Before Service Meetings," in this chapter.)

2. Communicate with pastoral staff person in charge of altar workers *regularly* regarding special announcements, altar worker program changes, special meetings.

3. Follow up on absentee altar workers.

4. One leader or captain is to be put in charge of checking the prayer room for supplies of *all* materials and then notifying the staff of any inventory needs.

5. Give written and oral tests to trainees.

6. Anything else you might think of!

USE THE "BUDDY SYSTEM"
•••

After trainees have passed the written and oral tests to become new altar workers, each of them should accompany an experienced altar worker (or service captain) into the prayer room. Then they can see how what they have learned is to be shared in a real situation.

They should do this twice. The third time, the new workers should be allowed to share while the experienced workers listen. Afterwards, the experienced ones can critique the new workers (trainees). Later on, they can discuss the progress of the new workers with the service captain or leader. If the new workers did well, they can be released to work on their own with the approval of the head altar worker.

"BEFORE SERVICE MEETINGS"
•••

A time of prayer and communication before each service is strongly recommended as part of the altar worker program. (See point 6 under "Qualifications for All Helps Ministries Workers" in a following chapter.)

These brief meetings allow leaders to do the following:

1. Pray for souls to be won, for prodigals to come home, for people to be filled with the Spirit. Pray for the pastor or speaker to be anointed and for the altar workers to flow with God. (Approximately ten minutes of prayer.)

2. Take attendance in order to know who shows up. The service leader or captain may occasionally want to follow up on the absentees just to let them know they are cared for.

3. Rearrange order of altar workers' response to the altar call to compensate for absentees.

4. Communicate any special announcements affecting the altar workers.

5. Make sure Follow-up Report forms, writing boards and pens are set on chairs in the prayer room or designated area.

6. Make sure there are enough ministry packets ready to hand out to respondents.

7. Make preparations for a large response by assigning workers appropriate tasks if it is necessary to use Plan B.

   Leaders may want to use this list as a format for their "Before Service Meetings."

Guidelines for Altar Workers
• • •

The following samples of guidelines, requirements and procedures have been included for leaders to adapt and use at their churches. A final copy should be made for each altar worker.

ALTAR WORKER'S PURPOSE
• • •

Your purpose as an altar worker is to assure all those who respond to an altar call at (your church's name) that they have received from the Lord what they came for. It is of utmost importance that respondents be pointed to Jesus and to God's Word as the Source for supplying their need.

As an altar worker at (your church's name), you will be sharing with the respondents about three subjects: salvation, restoration and the baptism in the Holy Spirit. It is vital that you not go beyond these three areas. Any counseling needs are to be referred to the specified staff member(s).

The respondents must know and understand that you, the worker, are not sharing your own opinions, but are sharing what God's Word says by using the Bible during your time together.

Your time with a respondent should be from ten to no more than twenty minutes in length. Your goal is to give this person a good, basic understanding as is necessary in these three areas.

ALTAR WORKER REQUIREMENTS

1. Must be a member of (your church's name), or plan to enroll in its next available series of membership classes, and be attending your church regularly.

2. Must fill out and sign a Helps Ministry Application and qualify for service.

3. Must agree to operate in this ministry within the prescribed guidelines, always in harmony with pastoral direction.

   Optional: Make workers aware that disciplinary suspensions are a part of the altar worker program at (your church's name).

4. Must agree to follow-up requirements. A personal phone call or visit with the respondent(s) ministered to in the previous service must be made within the first forty-eight hours. Ladies without a partner are excepted, but they must contact their respondent(s) by phone.

   Important: this is subject to your current follow-up program. If you have follow-up teams, inform the person that he/she will be contacted soon by someone else from your church and will be provided with other information.

5. Must make a follow-up call one week later after the original follow-up contact.

6. Must arrive at church twenty minutes prior to the start of the service to participate in intercessory prayer in the

prayer room. (List time of services here. Example: 10:40 A.M. Sunday; 6:40 P.M. Wednesday.)

7. Must be diligent in maintaining the highest standards of personal hygiene. (*No body odor!*)

8. Must have fresh breath, so make sure breath mints are available.

9. Must maintain a neat appearance.

Men: Hair combed; clean shaven; mustache and/or beard neatly trimmed; wearing dress pants, dress shirt and tie.

Women: Hair combed; wearing dress or skirt and blouse.

Note: All clothing should be neatly pressed.

10. Men to pray with men; women to pray with women.

Scheduling

1. Each month you will receive the schedule for the following month before the first service of that month. Please make note of the services you are scheduled to work.

Important: Note the order in which workers' names are listed. This is the order in which they are to respond during the altar call. For example, the first female worker on the list goes forward when the first female respondent comes forward; the fifth male worker listed goes forward when the fifth male respondent comes forward. Only the workers listed will be expected to work that week unless other duties are assigned them.

Please read any announcements that follow on the schedule itself. These are an important means of communication.

2. You must agree that if unable to attend your scheduled time, you will make the necessary contacts with another worker to secure a replacement. A phone list will be provided.

ALTAR WORKER PROCEDURES
• • •

Before Service:

Attend "Before Service Meetings" when you are scheduled to work.

During Service:

Sit in the section reserved for altar workers during the service in which you are working. (Note: the section reserved for altar workers should give you a good view of the front with easy access to it.)

A badge will be provided and must be worn at each service in which you are working.

React immediately to the altar call in the order that you are listed on the schedule by walking to the front when those who respond come forward. Don't wait to be called by Pastor ___[last name]___. Remember: men with men, women with women.

Accompany respondents to the prayer room. [If your church does not have a prayer room, you are to go to the area designated by your leader.]

PRAYER ROOM PROCEDURE
• • •

We have included two plans to be used by altar workers to cover prayer room situations, depending on the number of people responding to the altar call. (Follow-up Reports, writing boards and pens should already be laid out on some of the chairs.)

Plan A:

As an altar worker, you should introduce yourself to the respondent you stood behind as you lead him/her to a chair that has a Follow-up Report form and ask him/her to be seated. Take the form from the chair and place it under your seat. Be sure to keep the same momentum as was in the service! Remember, the quicker you can share everything with them, the better.

Ask respondents why they answered the altar call. Keeping their comments in mind, pick up where the speaker left off. If the respondents were already led in the sinner's prayer, you need not go over that again; you can go on then to the baptism in the Holy Spirit. If they were not led in the sinner's prayer, share with them about salvation and the baptism in the Holy Spirit. Remember that you are not trying to convince them; they have already made a decision.

Those who responded for restoration should be ministered to and then asked this *most important* question: "Have you received the baptism in the Holy Spirit since you believed, and do you speak with tongues?" People will often respond, "I have been baptized." You must clarify what you mean — that you are not referring to water baptism — then ask them again.

After this, lead respondents in an appropriate prayer and conclude that part of your time together. If they ask any questions, you may answer them — but only briefly.

Take the Follow-up Report from beneath your chair. Tell the respondents to fill out the appropriate sections *completely*, asking them to press hard and write big.

Ask the respondents if they have a Bible. If they don't, tell them the church would like to give them one. Then excuse yourself to get the materials they need, those items that are applicable to their situation. If packets have been made up, individual books should also be available; not everyone will need all that is included in the packet.

I would suggest respondents be given a combination of materials, such as booklets by Kenneth E. Hagin[1] and handouts I have written (and included in this book)[2] as listed below:

A. Salvation/Holy Spirit Baptism:

"Your Next Steps" handout

The New Birth

Why Tongues? and/or *The Bible Way To Receive the Holy Spirit*

In Him

"What About Water Baptism?" handout

Redeemed

B. Baptism in the Holy Spirit:

Why Tongues? and/or *The Bible Way To Receive the Holy Spirit*

---

[1] These books may be obtained at your local Christian bookstore or by writing Kenneth Hagin Ministries for information about ordering. The ministry address is P. O. Box 50126, Tulsa, OK 74150-0126. To place VISA or MasterCard orders, call 1-800-54-FAITH.

[2] You may photocopy "Your Next Steps" and "What About Water Baptism?" from this book to distribute as handouts; or better yet, have them professionally printed with your church's name and logo.

C. Restoration:

"Your Next Steps" handout

In Him

Redeemed

"What About Water Baptism?" handout (if respondents have not yet been obedient in this)

The handout materials listed here are ones I have found to be quite good. But there are a multitude of excellent materials. Pick what works well for you. Also, you will need to have Bibles (at least New Testaments) available to give to those who may not have a Bible. I suggest the *New King James Version*.

After returning to the respondents with the materials they need, check over the Follow-up Report form they have filled out to make sure it has been completed. Question them about any uncompleted portion and fill it in yourself.

Ask respondents when would be a good time within the next two days for you to give them a call or stop by for a visit. Try to commit to a specific time to contact them — and stick to it!

Put the Follow-up Report form aside. Then point out the packet of materials you have for the respondents, briefly telling them what is covered in each of the materials. Stress the handout, "Your Next Steps," to those who have just received the Lord and also to those who have sought restoration. Encourage them to read through it first, then go on to the other materials.

After a quick overview of the value and content of the materials being given to the respondents, your overview on the church's handout materials should not take more than a minute per item. Keep in mind that the person or persons to whom you are talking may, by now, be getting anxious about relatives, friends or lunch. You should pray a brief closing prayer with them.

Scripture is clear. As Jesus said in Mark 4:15, the enemy will come to try to steal the Word from their heart. In your prayer, be sure to thank the Lord for what He has done in the respondent's life. This also gives you another opportunity to briefly share the highlights of what you have previously discussed in your time together. Your prayer could go something like this:

For Salvation:

Dear heavenly Father, we come to You in Jesus' name. I thank You for (person's name), my new brother/sister in the Lord. I rejoice with him/her and with the angels that he/she is saved. He/she is now born again and is a new member of the family of God.

I pray that in the days ahead Your Spirit will live big in them, that He will open the eyes of their understanding and they might know what is the hope of their calling. According to Your mighty power, I ask You to strengthen them with might by Your Spirit in their inner man. And, Satan, I bind you in Jesus' name from stealing the Word of God, which has been sown in their heart.

[If applicable:] Dear Jesus, I thank You for filling them with the Holy Spirit and His power to be a witness and for giving them their new language. I release them into Your care, thanking You that the best days of (person's name) are ahead as he/she seeks to know You by reading Your Word, by worshiping You and by spending time with You daily in prayer. In Jesus' precious name. Amen!

For Restoration:

Dear heavenly Father, thank You for sending Jesus. Thank You that (person's name) is restored to fellowship with You. Satan, I bind you now from stealing the Word sown in his/her heart, in Jesus' name.

Father, thank You that there is now no condemnation to those who are in Christ Jesus. I pray for (person's name) and ask You to open the eyes of his/her understanding that he/she might know what is the hope of his/her calling, according to Your mighty power.

I ask You, in Jesus' name, to strengthen them with might by Your Spirit in their inner man. Lord, they are now cleansed. [If applicable:] Thank You for filling them with the Holy Spirit and His power to be a witness and for giving them their new language.

I release (person's name) into Your care now, and I thank You that his/her best days are ahead as he/she continues to seek to know You by reading Your Word, by worshiping You and by spending time with You daily in prayer. In Jesus' name, I pray. Amen.

For Baptism in the Holy Spirit:

Dear heavenly Father, thank You for sending Jesus. Thank You that (person's name) is saved and that heaven is his/her home.

Thank You, Father, for filling them with the precious Holy Spirit and for giving them the power they need to be a witness for You. Thank You for giving them their new language. It will be such a blessing to them as they are diligent to use it, praying daily to You.

Lord, I thank You that the best days of (person's name) are ahead as he/she continues to seek You by reading Your Word, by worshiping You and by spending time with You daily in prayer. In Jesus' name. Amen.

. . . .

Remind the respondents that you will be in touch, then release them to go.

Be sure to complete the "Prayer Room Worker's Information" section of the Follow-up Report form, then sign it and date it. Remember to keep your copy for follow-up, but turn in the church's copy to the designated area.

Make sure you follow up according to your church's program.

Plan B, Large Crowd Response (when twelve or more people respond to the altar call):

1. The leader or service captain will direct the respondents to the prayer room or other designated area, with the assistance of workers who have been preappointed by the leader to assist them.

   [This prayer room or designated area should be prepared ahead of time when you have evangelistic-type services. In other situations, when it becomes clear that Plan B will have to be used, immediately release the preappointed workers to ready the room. The leader or service captain should assign workers during the "Before Service Meetings" to set up chairs around the wall, if that is not your normal practice; to assemble packets; and to place Follow-up Reports with pens and boards on the chairs.]

2. The leader or service captain will assign altar workers to act as ushers, directing the respondents into lines facing a raised platform (or chair) on which the leader or service captain is standing in order to address the crowd.

3. After all respondents have entered the room, the altar workers should enter and stand behind them. If limited space in the back of the room requires it, they may form lines along the side walls.

4. The leader or service captain will address the respondents at the point where the speaker or pastor left off, keeping the same momentum as was in the service.

   A. Let the respondents know you are excited about their decision. Tell them they have opened the door to God for Him to move on their behalf and it's the best decision they have ever made.

   B. Minister in any of the three areas not covered by the speaker or pastor. For instance, you will generally start with salvation and lead them in an appropriate prayer. If the prayer of salvation has already been prayed with a prayer of restoration included, you should lead them similarly as follows:

   "According to God's Holy Word, you are now saved or restored in your relationship to God. [Quote Romans 10:9,10.] To those of you who came forward for restoration, 1 John 1:9 says, [quote it]."

   Then lead the respondents in a prayer similar to this:

   "Thank You, Lord, that I am now saved. The Word says my sins are forgiven, so I am now in a relationship with You. I am Your child. Heaven is my home. You have made me the righteousness of God in Christ. In Jesus' name. Amen."

Then say to them:

"Now there is a second experience God has for you. Jesus told the disciples in Acts 1:4,5 to wait for the baptism in the Holy Spirit. [Quote Acts 1:8; 2:1-4.] In Mark 16:17 Jesus said one of the signs that will follow believers is, 'In My name they shall speak in new tongues.' Jesus commanded His disciples to wait for this, and He is now speaking to you! If you have not yet received this gift, please raise your hands. Thank you. Now keep them up."

LEADERSHIP: At this point there are two options for you to choose from as to how you will proceed. You may continue to minister to the entire group of respondents about the baptism in the Holy Spirit. Upon completion, you would release them to fill out the Follow-up Report with the assistance of the altar workers. Or, you can release to go those who have already been filled with the Holy Spirit and speak in tongues and have them to fill out the Follow-up Report while the service captain or leader shares with those who have not yet received. The latter is the method given in these guidelines.

"Those of you who have received the baptism in the Holy Spirit and speak in tongues, please go to the chairs and fill out the forms that have been placed there. Press hard, write big and fill them out completely. Then take your completed forms outside where we have something to give you. An altar worker will be available to assist you.

"Those of you with your hands raised, please step forward. [Quote Luke 11:9-13.] You see, the Bible says that to receive this gift you simply need to ask for it. It also says that, when you ask for something from the Lord, you must believe that you receive *when* you ask. So, when I lead you in asking for this gift, you will receive right now!

"In Acts, chapters 8 and 19, the disciples laid hands on those who desired to receive the baptism in the Holy Spirit. I am going to lead you in asking the Lord for this gift. When we finish, the altar workers will come and lay their hands on you. The moment they do, you will receive, so you can expect to speak in tongues right then. You should immediately begin to speak loudly enough that you can hear yourself with your own ears, but don't speak in English — or we could say, with your understanding. The words will come from down inside you, not from your mind. An altar worker will be helping you. Now let's pray:

"Dear heavenly Father, thank You for my salvation. Your Word tells me that if I ask for it, You will fill me with the Holy Spirit and I will receive power to be a witness for You and also a new language. So I ask You right now to baptize me with the Holy Spirit. Thank You for it, Father. I expect to be filled and to speak in other tongues the moment hands are laid on me. In Jesus' name. Amen!"

Upon completion of your prayer, you will then release the altar workers who are available to lay hands on those receiving.

ALTAR WORKERS: You should not take too long with anyone. There may be many people needing to have hands laid on them as a point of contact to help them release their faith to receive. If they are struggling and/or you cannot get them to speak, you should politely excuse yourself by saying something like: "I am going to move on to the next person, but I will return to help you as soon as I can. Begin to say thank You to the Lord for baptizing you in the Holy Spirit. Worship the Lord. I will be with you again shortly." Then move on to the next person.

5. After everyone has had hands laid on them, direct the respondents to chairs where they are to fill out a Follow-up Report. Be sure to tell them to press hard, write big and fill out the form completely.

6. Have altar workers assist the respondents. When the forms have been completed, direct them to where the forms will be recorded and collected.

7. After the forms are collected, direct the respondents to a table located outside the room where they will receive a packet which includes the following: "Your Next Steps" handout, *In Him, Why Tongues?, The New Birth* and "What About Water Baptism?" handout (if needed).

8. All altar workers are to remain in the room until they receive a copy of the form(s) they are to follow up on.

9. Altar workers must call upon the respondents, whose names have been given to them. They are to introduce themselves and proceed with the standard follow-up.

Within three days, they must return the Follow-up Reports to the prayer room or designated area.

10. All altar workers available at the time of need should, if at all possible, respond to large altar calls in any service.

Plan B: Room Setup Guidelines

• Chairs are to be placed along the walls.

• Materials are to be provided, such as ministry packets and Bibles (packets work best at this time).

• Platform (or chair) on which speaker is to stand is to be placed at one end of the room.

• Have a table or two available for quick setup.

Some of this can and should be done in advance of the service. At least the chairs can be set up and table(s) made ready.

Although these guidelines are for large responses, you may certainly use them as your standard prayer room setup.

Plan B: Instructions to Altar Workers

Unless you are involved in setting up the prayer room or are helping to usher, do not enter the room until all the respondents are inside. Stand in the back or, if space limitations require, stand in front of the chairs along the side walls. At the appropriate time, follow any instructions given by the service captain or leader. Please be as quiet as possible so as not to distract the respondents' attention away from the speaker.

Those workers assigned to set up the room should be finishing their tasks as quietly as possible.

Be ready either to assist respondents in filling out the Follow-up Reports completely or to assist those receiving the baptism in the Holy Spirit, or both if necessary.

If at all possible, all altar workers present in the service, though not scheduled, should respond to large altar calls, mainly to help with follow-up. Workers should *not* leave when the respondents do.

All Follow-up Report forms must be recorded, then distributed to workers for follow-up calls. Workers should take more than one form if asked to do so and make the necessary calls. If possible, they should introduce themselves to their respondents and follow the standard procedures for follow-up calls.

Upon completion of the follow-ups, the workers are to return these forms to the designated area. They must be sure this information is recorded on the Altar Worker Record Sheet (see sample forms in a later chapter).

Ministry in the Prayer Room:
The Specifics
• • •

The following procedures have been included for leaders to adapt and use at their churches. A copy should be made for each altar worker.

How To Minister on Salvation: Simply!
• • •

This is the method I use. I would suggest, however, that your church utilize *one standard method* to ensure that your workers recognize what they are to share. The following is just one of *many* possible series of Scripture verses that are applicable.

If the pastor has not led respondents in the sinner's prayer, it is up to the altar workers to do so.

John 3:16

Romans 3:23

Romans 5:8

Romans 6:23

Ephesians 2:8,9

Romans 10:9,10

As an altar worker, you should turn to these verses in your Bible and read them as you go. Remember that you should keep the same momentum as was in the church service and that you should keep it as short as possible, no more than twenty minutes. Your message to the respondent might go like this:

"(Person's name), look at what the Bible says: **For God so loved the world, that he gave his only begotten Son, that whosoever believeth in him should not perish, but have everlasting life.** God sent Jesus to die for you, because **all have sinned, and come short of the glory of God.**

"(Person's name), you have sinned, but Scripture says, **God commendeth** (or showed) **his love toward us, in that, while we were yet sinners, Christ died for us.** It says: **The wages of sin is death; but the gift of God is eternal life through Jesus Christ our Lord.** We cannot work or earn our way to heaven. **For by grace are ye saved through faith; and that not of yourselves: it is the gift of God: not of works, lest any man should boast.** But Scripture also says: **If thou shalt confess with thy mouth the Lord Jesus, and shalt believe in thine heart that God hath raised him from the dead, thou shalt be saved. For with the heart man believeth unto righteousness; and with the mouth confession is made unto salvation.**"

It is most important that, as you go through this process, you read and show each Scripture to the respondent. Let it flow. Pause only when you need to look up the next Scripture. Be sure to maintain eye contact with the respondent.

If you know where you are headed, it will go quickly and smoothly, and you will save a great deal of time. Remember, your goal during this time is not to convince respondents to be saved or filled. They have already decided to do that. Neither is it your job to give them a thorough knowledge of Scripture, but to help them see quickly what God says is the way for them to be saved, to be restored to fellowship or to be filled with the Holy Spirit.

Don't get sidetracked by spending a lot of time answering the respondent's questions. Just go through your presentation. If asked a question, you might reply: "I would be glad to answer your question in a few minutes, but our time is limited, so let's get through this first. All right?" If time permits, after the respondent becomes Spirit filled, you can briefly answer his/her question, as long as it pertains to doctrine or is relevant to your purpose.

You should not be answering questions that ask for your advice, such as, "What should I do?" If the respondent has a serious situation, politely excuse yourself, and go and tell your service captain or leader what has been said. Your leader can then deal with that person's problem by contacting a staff member, if necessary!

Important: If during this time, a respondent indicates being a victim of or says he/she is being tempted to do any of the following: physical abuse of any kind, child abuse of any kind, suicide or murder; you should follow these instructions and immediately excuse yourself to speak with your service captain or leader.

When you are finished with your church's presentation on salvation, ask respondents to repeat after you, saying to them:

"(Person's name), just pray this prayer after me: Dear God in heaven, thank You for sending Your Son Jesus to die for me and to pay for my sins. I believe You raised Him from the dead. Now, Jesus, I ask You to come into my heart and to cleanse me of my sins, to be my Lord and to make heaven my home. I now confess with my mouth that You, Jesus, are my Lord. Thank You, Father, that I am now saved. I have eternal life with You! In Jesus' name, I pray. Amen."

HOW TO MINISTER
THE BAPTISM IN THE HOLY SPIRIT:
IT'S EASY!
* * *

But First, Some Important Thoughts...

The second experience God has for every believer is to be filled with the Holy Spirit as evidenced by speaking in tongues. Getting believers filled with the Holy Spirit after they are born again is a command of the Lord. God wants every believer filled with the Holy Spirit for two reasons, just as He gave us His Word for two reasons (see Proverbs 22:19-21). God gave us His Word that we might KNOW the truth, and then SHARE the truth with others.

The first reason the Lord fills us with an additional measure of power is for *our benefit,* to help us live victorious lives. The second reason He fills us with His Spirit is for the benefit of others in the fulfilling of God's purpose on earth. We are a much better equipped "army for the Lord" when we are filled with His "power to be witnesses" (Acts 1:8) and can speak in tongues to build ourselves up in faith and to pray out the perfect will of God (Acts 2:4; 38,39; Jude 20; Romans 8:26,27; 1 Corinthians 14:2,4).

In Ephesians 5:18, we see that the Lord through the apostle Paul commands every believer to ...**be filled with the Spirit....** I think any Charismatic minister would agree that this promised infilling is a very important part of what the Lord wants every believer to receive.

The baptism in the Holy Spirit is not to be taken lightly Obviously, the Lord knew the difference the baptism in the Holy Spirit would make in the disciples' lives. So in Acts 1, He commanded them to tarry in Jerusalem in anticipation of receiving this gift. When they received the Holy Spirit, he equipped the disciples of the early church to take the Gospel to the world of their day. The same "Great Commission" that sent them from Judea into the uttermost parts of the world is still in force today. The Lord's desire to win the lost has not diminished.

Probably now more than ever, believers still need to receive the "power to be witnesses" (Acts 1:8) which is given by the Holy Spirit.

The apostle Paul wrote an in-depth discourse in 1 Corinthians 14 to help us better understand God's purpose for the evidence of the Holy Spirit's infilling, which is speaking in tongues. In this passage, he encourages believers to use the gift publicly in Church, as they are led by God "by two or three" as a sign to unbelievers (1 Corinthians 14:27). He also enlightens us concerning the private use of tongues for our own personal prayer time (1 Corinthians 14:2-4, 13-19, see also Romans 8:26-28).

Again, let me point out that in Ephesians 5:18, Paul instructs every believer to be filled with the Spirit. Therefore, in light of these Scriptures, I believe you can see why it should be a priority to see those who come to receive salvation, also receive the baptism in the Holy Spirit.

The next statement may seem too strong, but it is true. Since the Scriptures command us to be filled with the Holy Spirit, any believer who does not seek to be "filled" with the Holy Spirit as is recorded in Acts 2:4,38,89 is in disobedience to Jesus, the Head of the Church.

Whether one is unaware of the existence of this gift, or has been taught that this promised infilling is not for our dispensation, the truth remains: Jesus Christ commanded us to be filled with the Holy Spirit.

Please understand that I am not saying that the Lord will send a believer to hell for *not* receiving the baptism in the Holy Spirit. However, we should not take lightly what we have been given by the Lord. God has a purpose for everything He does. Therefore, whether by commission or omission, if we stop short of receiving all that God has for us, we are robbing the Lord of our full potential as "ambassadors for Christ" (2 Corinthians 5:18-20). We actually diminish God's ability to effectively proclaim the Gospel *through us* to a lost world.

WHEN TO OFFER THE "GIFT"
...

There is some variance in thought concerning the "best" time to share the baptism in the Holy Spirit with a newly born-again believer.

To settle that issue in your own mind, ask yourself this question: Should you give people in a congregation the opportunity to receive the gift on a regular basis, or should you devote special times to minister on the subject a few times every year?

To answer this question, let's consider these two predominate viewpoints. You can then prayerfully determine which direction the Lord wants you to follow.

WHY WAIT?
...

The first viewpoint supports sharing the baptism in the Holy Spirit immediately with new converts. I believe that this is the viewpoint most widely practiced.

Acts 8:14,15 tells us that Peter and John were sent to Samaria as soon as they heard that the Samaritans were receiving the Gospel. They went in haste to make sure that those new believers were "filled" with the Holy Spirit.

In Acts 10:44-47, we see believers receiving the baptism in the Holy spirit at the exact same time as they received their salvation. Obviously, the Lord wanted them to be filled immediately upon conversion.

In Acts 19:2, Paul asked disciples he met in Ephesus, **...Have ye received the Holy Ghost since ye believed?** When Paul laid hands on these men, everyone received the Holy Spirit, as evidenced by their "speaking in tongues." Here again, we see the baptism in the Holy Spirit being shared immediately after conversion.

Pastors, since the people in your congregation follow your lead, they need to see that you frequently place the same emphasis the Scriptures place on the gift of the Holy Spirit. If you do not emphasize its importance from your pulpit, your congregation will not view it as being important. You can emphasize the importance of the baptism in the Holy Spirit by teaching the subject on a regular basis and giving them the opportunity to receive it.

Offer the Gift at Every Altar Call!
• • •

Make the baptism in the Holy Spirit a part of every altar call. There are two good reasons for this.

First, in this way your flock will be consistently reminded of the importance of receiving the power of the Holy Spirit in their own lives. To do so will take a bit of time out of each service, but it will be time well spent.

Second, respondents to your altar calls will not be surprised when altar workers address the baptism in the Holy Spirit in the prayer room if the offer was extended from the pulpit. When is that important? Because some people responding to the altar call may not be willing to receive such ministry from your workers due to their different doctrinal beliefs in this area. If, however, you offer the baptism in the Holy Spirit each time you give an altar call, even first time visitors will know your doctrinal stance before they respond and enter the prayer room.

Something to consider about this approach is that your workers will need to spend more time in the prayer room with those desiring to receive the baptism in the Holy Spirit in order to answer any questions they might have. This means that their family and friends will have to wait longer for them. Another thing to consider about this approach is that you must be certain that your altar workers are *very, very well-trained* in this area, so they do not confuse or hinder the respondents from receiving the infilling of the Holy Spirit.

THEY WILL RECEIVE — IN TIME...
• • •

The other viewpoint regarding when to minister to the baptism in the Holy Spirit is that a foundation must be laid before the "gift of the Holy Spirit" should be offered. Then an altar call ban be given for that specific purpose.

Pastors, by teaching about it *before* giving an altar call for the baptism in the Holy Spirit, you build a foundation for faith in those who hear the message. Then, they are spiritually ready to receive what God has for them. For example, Jesus taught first, and then healed the people. This perspective is based on the true belief that, **Faith cometh by hearing, and hearing by the word of God** (Romans 10:17).

If this is the way you are led, Pastor, be open to teaching on the subject regularly throughout the year.

The main advantage to this method is that after hearing an in-depth teaching on the subject, each respondents faith level will rise, making it easy to receive this gift from the Lord.

Also, another point to consider is that this method will cut down on the time each respondent will spend in the prayer room.

IT'S YOUR CHOICE, PASTOR
• • •

Selecting the best method to use in ministering the baptism in the Holy Spirit during regular services in your church is a decision to be made by the church leadership.

In my opinion, Pastor, both viewpoints can and should be practiced at the same time. Offer the baptism in the Holy Spirit at each service and also teach specifically about the subject three or four times a year, giving an altar call specifically for the baptism in the Holy Spirit.

Important Note: The following guidelines have been written with the perspective in mind that you will be giving individuals the opportunity at every service to receive the baptism in the Holy Spirit.

Ministering the Baptism in the Holy Spirit

After the person you are ministering to has prayed the prayer of salvation, go right on to the baptism in the Holy Spirit. Scriptures to be shared are: Acts 1:4,5,8; 2:1,4,38,39; Luke 11:9,10a,13; Mark 16:17.

Using your Bible, turn to these Scripture verses and read them as you go. Your message to the respondent might be as follows:

"(Person's name), as you know, God the Father sent, or gave us, His Son! Jesus now wants to give you a gift as well, which the Bible calls the baptism in the Holy Spirit.

"After Jesus was resurrected, He instructed His disciples to **wait for the promise of the Father, which, saith he, ye have heard of me. For John truly baptized with water; but ye shall be baptized with the Holy Ghost not many days hence.... But ye shall receive power, after that the Holy Ghost is come upon you: and ye shall be witnesses unto me both in Jerusalem, and in all Judaea, and in Samaria, and unto the uttermost part of the earth.**

"Then Scripture says, **When the day of Pentecost was fully come, they were all with one accord in one place...And they were all filled with the Holy Ghost and** (they) **began to speak with other tongues, as the Spirit gave them utterance** (or words).

"Then Peter said unto them, Repent, and be baptized every one of you in the name of Jesus Christ for the remission of sins, and ye shall receive the gift of the Holy Ghost. For the promise is unto you, and to your children, and to all that are afar off, even as many as the Lord our God shall call.

"Jesus said, Ask, and it shall given you; seek, and ye shall find; knock, and it shall be opened unto you. For every one that asketh receiveth...how much more shall your heavenly Father give the Holy Spirit to them that ask him? These signs shall follow them that believe; In my name...they shall speak with new tongues. Notice Jesus said that *everyone* who asked received.

"As you can see from the Bible, God has promised this gift to you now that you are saved! Can you see that?"

If respondents answer yes, go on.

If they answer no, ask them a question. Begin by saying: "I know I haven't been able to spend much time sharing this with you. Is there some part of what I shared that I could go over again?" Answer their question(s) *briefly,* then say something like: "Did that help you understand better?"

If they still answer no, or if you are at the end of your designated time (twenty minutes), excuse yourself for a moment. Find your service captain (or other leader) and introduce that person to the respondent. Explain out loud what you have discussed, then let your leader take it from there.

At this point candidates for the baptism in the Holy Spirit should understand the following:

- What the baptism in the Holy Spirit is and what accompanies it: power to be a witness for the Lord; a new spiritual language.

- That it is promised to them, that God wants them to receive it.

- That they receive by asking for it (Luke 11:13).

Ask them again if they understand and if they would like to receive.

If they do not, go ahead and finish the time you have together by completing the Follow-up Report and giving them the appropriate materials. Then encourage them by saying something like this:

"(Person's name), I am very excited for you. You are now saved (or restored into fellowship with the Lord). Don't be concerned about not receiving the baptism in the Holy Spirit. Your understanding will grow. We have included in your packet the booklet *Why Tongues?*, and we believe it will help you. I will be calling you, and if any more questions arise, I will try to answer them. You will receive in time."

At this point let them leave. Then you are to do your normal follow-up at the appropriate time.

Laying Hands on Them To Receive

When you asked if they wanted to receive and they answered yes, you should proceed, making sure they understand the following as you lead them in a prayer, then lay hands on them to receive:

- They should release their faith when hands are laid on them. If *they* ask, they *will* receive.

- *They* have to speak out loud. The Holy Spirit won't move their tongue for them. It's just like deciding to say anything else out loud: if *they* don't speak, it won't be said.

- The utterance words will rise up from down inside them, from their "belly" (John 7:38).

- They don't have to understand it! It is a spiritual language.

  You should say something like this: "(Person's name), I would like to pray with you and lay hands on you just as the Bible says to do." If they are hesitant, follow the same procedure as before.

- Ask them *tactfully* what they don't understand.

- Answer by going over what the Bible says about what they don't understand.

- Ask them, "Are you ready to receive now?"

- If they say yes, go ahead and pray.

- If they say no, see about getting some assistance from an approved person (as specified in your church's instructions).

Remind them that you will place your hands on their head and/or shoulders after you have prayed together. Then they should release their faith, believing at that moment that God is filling them. They should speak out loud in their new language.

As you are leading them in prayer, have them repeat after you words similar to this:

"Dear heavenly Father, I thank You that I am saved, that heaven is my home and Jesus is my Lord. You promised You would baptize Your children in the Holy Spirit. Lord Jesus,

I ask You now to give me the Holy Spirit, and I receive Him by faith. I believe when (altar worker's name) lays hands on me, I will be filled with the Holy Spirit and I will speak out boldly in my new language. In Jesus' name. Amen."

You should then lay hands on them and pray out loud in your own spiritual language. Pray loud enough for them to hear, but don't drown them out. As you are speaking, be listening for them to speak.

- If they are speaking softly, encourage them to be a little louder.

- If they still do not speak, go through the questions shared earlier and try again.

- If they still aren't speaking, you may want to ask for assistance.

If they have not yet spoken in tongues, let them know:

- That they have received since they asked. God's Word says, **Ask, and it shall be given you** (Matthew 7:7).

- That they *can* speak in tongues, but that *they* must do it, or it won't happen.

- That God wants them to use the gift He has given them.

- That they are not to be discouraged.

Work with the respondents on your follow-up and try to help them some more.

Encourage them strongly to read the books you have given them about the baptism in the Holy Spirit.

When They *Do* Speak in Tongues

Once the respondents have spoken out loud in their prayer language, encourage them to pray daily using their new language and to pray also in their understanding (probably English). Let them know they don't need to have some special feeling or to be in a certain place in order to pray in tongues; they control its usage. To illustrate this, have them pray out loud with you in tongues for another minute or two.

Remember, the more natural and simple you make it — after all, it is the normal course in the plan of God for their lives — the easier it will be to help them receive. Don't make it mysterious or spooky. To avoid that, *you* must be convinced that it is not mysterious or spooky, that it isn't hard to lead someone in receiving the baptism in the Holy Spirit.

Even if the pastor or leader does not give books by Kenneth E. Hagin to their new converts, I highly recommend that they have their altar workers read and study his minibook, *The Bible Way To Receive the Holy Spirit.* It will bless them.

MINISTERING RESTORATION:
HELP THEM UNDERSTAND!
• • •

Restoration is simple. The altar worker's goal here is to help respondents leave the prayer room knowing they are *restored to fellowship* with God.

It might be good, however, to remind them that, even though they may have sinned or backslidden and it may have been some time since they were in fellowship with God, they are still in relationship with Him. My sons are still my sons, whether they obey me or not.

A Prayer of Restoration

You should say something like this to the respondents:

"When you turned away from the Lord, you broke your fellowship with Him, but not your relationship. Children don't become orphans because they disobey their parents. They just need to be confronted and disciplined in love to restore their fellowship with their parents.

"God says the way for us to be restored is: **If we confess our sins, he is faithful and just to forgive us our sins, and to cleanse us from all unrighteousness.** That is 1 John 1:9.

"Now let's pray together. When it's time for you to confess your sins, I will squeeze your hand. Then you should talk to God quietly on the inside and confess your sins to Him. When you are finished, squeeze my hand, then I will continue leading you in prayer. So pray this prayer after me:

"Dear heavenly Father, I come to You in Jesus' name. According to 1 John 1:9, I confess that I have sinned. [Have the respondent confess *silently* what is on his/her heart.] Now, Father, I accept by faith my cleansing and forgiveness from You, and I forgive myself by faith. I purpose to walk in Your ways. Thank You that I am clean before You, that I have been restored to fellowship with You. In Jesus' name. Amen."

At this point you should ask respondents if they have received the baptism in the Holy Spirit.

If they respond no, you can share it with them.

If they respond yes, encourage them to pray in their prayer language as a way of edifying and building themselves up. To make sure they have a good flow in their prayer language, ask to pray together with them for a minute in tongues. If all is well, go on to the Follow-up Report. If there is a problem, help them get a release in their language by going over the scriptural basics with them.

BE ASSERTIVE, NOT AGGRESSIVE
...

When you are in the prayer room as an altar worker, you need to keep control of your conversation with the respondent. You have been given a job to do, but there isn't much time to do it.

You keep control by being assertive. To assert is to insist on being recognized, to thrust oneself forward. In the prayer room you as an altar worker have the responsibility to communicate with respondents the truths they are seeking. The time is limited, as you know, so you need to control your time together. You should be doing most of the talking.

Emotions can run high during this time period, and I understand that. However, you must not allow that to keep you from communicating with them. You have an important message to share, and they need it.

People may want to display their emotions, but the environment will help to some degree. No matter how much guilt or sorrow may be going on inside most people, they will put on their "natural brakes" when they find themselves in a room full of strangers.

If, however, you find you are with people who are ruled strongly by emotions, think of yourself as a shock absorber. Be a calming influence. Get them a tissue if they need it. Be supportive. Slowly move into your message on a positive note. The apostle Paul always started out his letters to the churches with a word of encouragement. But he was used frequently by the Holy Spirit to follow that word of encouragement with a correction of their errors.

Fortunately, correcting error is not a part of altar work, except when dealing with any differences about what you are sharing — salvation, restoration and the baptism in the Holy Spirit — and what the respondents have understood in the past to be true about these subjects.

If questions arise about your church's doctrines on these three subjects, don't argue. Share calmly. Be assertive and steer them into an understanding of what you are saying, even if they don't agree at this time. If there is a persistent problem, ask for some help.

Being assertive is not being aggressive. Aggressive, defined in its negative connotation, means being boldly hostile or quarrelsome. Don't allow yourself to get upset at anyone. Get assistance if you start to become angry. People who come to the prayer room can occasionally be aggressive, but that's the rarity, not the norm.

I remember one time when I was sharing with a respondent. He became visibly upset when I questioned his understanding of what I had shared with him about the baptism in the Holy Spirit. Perhaps I pricked his pride. The old expression *If looks could kill* came to mind. This person had just been released from maximum-security prison, so I could understand his response to what I was saying. Rather than allowing our time to get misused by majoring on a misunderstanding, I redirected his attention to the important issue at hand: his salvation.

To be assertive, you need to know what the purpose of your time with respondents is, and what it is not. Keep focused on that.

Don't allow yourself to get sidetracked. Some issues just can't be solved or corrected in the brief time you have together, even if you could deal specifically with people's problems by "counseling" them.

Help people leave the prayer room knowing they are in relationship and fellowship with God, or as some might say, they are "right with God." If they weren't filled with the Holy Spirit before they came in, help them to leave filled. If they have shared their problems, you may recommend a need for counseling, but don't take on any more responsibility than that.

As an altar worker, you are to help the people with whom you share. You can do this more by being assertive and taking control than by allowing them to leave the time you have spent together without gaining the understanding of your message to them from God's Word.

This may take some time to develop, depending upon a variety of things, i.e., your personality type, your confidence level. The amount of experience you have had in altar working also plays a part. Consider these questions:

- Are you naturally assertive, or are you more of a timid or shy person?

- Do you know your material well?

- How many times have you done this kind of work?

The way you answer these questions will have an effect on you.

The good news is that, regardless of your personality type and whether this comes easily or is difficult for you, being assertive is certainly a good skill to have in every area of your life, as long as you are right. The message you have as an altar worker is right. It needs to be shared not only in the prayer room but in your everyday life with associates on any level.

Being an altar worker is a skill, and it can be developed. So make the effort. The rewards are great, both now and eternally.

Follow-up Is Essential
•••

This chapter details an aspect of altar working that goes above and beyond just working in the confines of a church service.

One of the greatest, most sacrificial and life-changing things altar workers can do for anyone is to pray for that person. After the respondents have left the prayer room, it is important that they be prayed for *daily!* (See 1 Samuel 12:23a; Ephesians 1:15,16; Galatians 4:19.)

I recommend the prayers Paul prayed for the church at Ephesus: Ephesians 1:17-23 and 3:14-21. These are foundation-building prayers, and the Holy Spirit inspired them as prayers to be prayed by us for others. (Every believer really should be praying these prayers daily for themselves as well.)

The altar workers should pray specifically for the respondents they have dealt with, and the rest of the respondents in general. Prayer is an integral part of the altar-working ministry, so they should do it!

FOLLOW-UP ON ALTAR CALL RESPONDENTS
• • •

Follow-up procedures will vary depending upon each church's established discipling program. The leaders will need to build the bridge between what their altar workers begin with in the prayer room and what they end with in their efforts to make disciples out of new converts.

SAMPLE GUIDELINES FOR FOLLOW-UP
• • •

The following procedures have been included for leaders to adapt and use at their churches. A copy of their final version should be made for each altar worker.

48-Hour Follow-up Guidelines

This is of utmost importance. Hopefully, you as an altar worker will have set up an appointment with the people you have ministered to before they have left the prayer room. Keep your appointment with them! Call them or visit them. During your time with them in person or on the phone, be sure you do the following:

1. Thank them for their response to the altar call.

2. Encourage them to know they made the best decision of their life.

3. Ask if they have read the material you gave them in the prayer room. If they have not, encourage them to do so, starting with the handout, "Your Next Steps," or whatever is most applicable.

4. Share briefly about the need for them to become active in their Christian life. You may want to start out by saying, "(Person's name), the reason I called (or came

by) is that I have some important things to share with you." Using "Your Next Steps" handout as a guide to prompt you, talk with them about their need to:

A. Read the Bible daily, specifically the New Testament. The gospel of John is a good place to start.

B. Pray daily, which is talking to God in Jesus' name, in English and in tongues; and worship and praise God daily.

C. Forsake their old manner of life.

D. Be water baptized. Let them know when the next water baptism service will be held at your church.

E. Support God's work financially at least by tithing.

F. Share Jesus with others and invite their friends and associates to church.

G. Attend church regularly.

H. Attend new believers' classes. Give them any available printed material on those classes.

Thank them for their time and tell them you will call within a week or ten days to see how they are doing.

Pray a closing prayer similar to the one you prayed with them in the prayer room.

Important: Be sure to fill out the white copy of the Follow-up Report with comments on your visit and return it to your church at the *next* service. Fill out your Altar Worker Record Sheet with the information you need for your follow-up callback to them in seven to ten days. (Example of Altar Worker Record Sheet is given in a later chapter.)

Follow-up Procedures If Plan B Is Used

When respondents outnumber altar workers, they still need follow-up. So the workers should make calls, not visits, to all those who filled out a Follow-up Report form.

After the respondents have left the prayer room, workers are to remain. The number of respondents should be evened out among the workers, with the Follow-up Report forms distributed accordingly.

Scheduling Your Workers
• • •

Leader, for ease of scheduling Plan A, get a computer! If not, try Plan B.

Plan B: Using a Master Schedule
• • •

With the Lord's help, I have put together a simple and easy system for you to use to schedule your altar workers when you are without a computer. You will need to make up the items listed below. You can draw the lines, and yes, you *can* use a computer if you have one!

• Altar Worker Availability Report

• Altar Worker Master Schedule, based on the number of services you have each week

   (See the chapter, "Sample Forms and Handouts," for samples.)

Simply take the information off the sample Availability Report and list the names of your workers on your Master Schedule in the appropriate boxes. Use that information for each service your workers are available to make up a monthly schedule.

You may prefer to schedule your workers as you need them rather than according to their availability. In some cases you may have to do this in order to meet the altar-working needs of your church. If you do so, be sure to inform your new workers from the beginning that they will be subject to your scheduling needs.

The new schedule should be in your altar workers' hands before the first service of the following month. Be sure to allow time for mailing or handing out so that each worker is given a copy in advance. To help you, I have included a sample Monthly Altar Worker Schedule (see the chapter, "Sample Forms and Handouts").

The sample schedule is based on a need to have five male workers and five female workers at the weekend services, and three male workers and three female workers at the midweek services. You will want to establish a similar requirement for your services based on your need, being mindful of Plan B if you are short of workers.

In Case of Absence

As was stated under the guidelines in chapter 3, if altar workers are unable to attend any service for which they have been scheduled, they are responsible for getting another person to cover for them.

The leaders must provide the workers with an accurate, up-to-date phone list. They might want to print this information on the back of each month's schedule. If, however, they are involved in a larger church with many workers, it would be better for them to make up a phone list separate from their schedule. This separate phone list should be updated at least twice a year.

Taking Attendance

Taking attendance will help both leaders and workers to know how successful they are at being faithful. A copy of the Altar Worker Schedule should be kept in the prayer room, and a check mark should be placed by the workers' names upon their arrival.

Soap Box

Leader, teaching your altar workers responsibility and accountability will bless them greatly. Since they are volunteers, you need to be an encourager.

Your workers come from a variety of backgrounds and circumstances, and they may not have been taught a good work ethic.

Using God's Word, you must encourage your workers to be faithful, i.e., loyal, conscientious, accurate and reliable; and to be diligent, i.e., persevering, careful in work, hard working. Teach them to commit, i.e., to bind as a promise, a pledge.

Commitment, diligence and faithfulness are principles that, if applied to the right circumstances, will bring great rewards.

If your altar workers do not show up for their regularly scheduled service and have not secured a replacement, call them to find out what is happening. If they fail to fulfill their commitment two or three times, you may choose to suspend them for a short time or to remove them from service.

SOME FINAL THOUGHTS
CONCERNING ALTAR WORKING

• • •

Water Baptism

Leader, you should have your workers strongly

encourage new converts to be water baptized. Have a regular water baptism service to accommodate them.

If your building does not have a baptistery, find another location.

Write your own pamphlet about water baptism or copy the one I have provided in the chapter, "Sample Forms and Handouts." Be sure everyone who responds to an altar call gets one of these handouts. It might surprise you how many believers have not yet followed the Lord's command in this.

Follow-up

Recognize that new converts are babies. They cannot and probably will not do much for themselves. Pastors, to the extent that you can, you need to have a system set up to help them make the right decisions over the next few weeks or months so they will establish good habits from the beginning in their relationship with God. Altar workers, you need to be faithful and diligent in the encouragement you give them in your follow-up.

Soap Box

God is the God of "full-circle revelation." What I mean is, He finishes where He starts. There are two examples for you to consider.

God placed Adam, the first man, in the Garden of Eden, which is believed to be located in the Middle East.[1] The world was populated outwardly from that geographic location. Now as we approach the end of this dispensation

---

[1] "In the absence of positive evidence, probability seems to point to the N. W. of Mesopotamia as the locality of Eden." William Smith, *Smith's Bible Dictionary*. (Old Tappan, NJ: Fleming H. Revell, 16th printing, May 1981), s.v. "Eden," p. 155.

of grace, the focus of the world's attention will be drawn back to the geographic location where everything started thousands of years ago.

The Body of Christ had its beginnings in the establishment of local churches as is clearly described in the book of Acts. Let's use this century as an example, because it is probably the one that will see the return of the Lord.

As we have seen in the 1940s, '50s, '60s and '70s, the Body of Christ has gone through several waves or moves of the Holy Spirit. During those years there occurred the Healing Revival, the Charismatic Movement and the Teaching Revival, respectively.

But now, more and more, the local church is the place God wants to use to build His kingdom. I am not saying the local church is the only way. The focus in these last days, however, will be on the local church.

Discipleship

Think of the local church as God's storehouse for the harvest. Every church has a different plan. One of the more popular plans has been home cell groups. But perhaps as a pastor or leader you have not been led to have these groups in your church.

This may be a little elementary, but as a brief reminder, you must recognize the need to set up a program of discipleship with the goal in mind of integrating your new converts into a lifestyle of church attendance. Provide within your church the activities necessary to promote relationships. This could include home gatherings, perhaps within the different areas of helps ministries, i.e., ushers, altar workers, children's workers. You can encourage your congregation with this as well, so that the local church becomes the heart of people's lives. In this sense it will meet the needs of every member regarding fellowship and socialization.

Home cell groups are great if that is what God has told you as the pastor to do. But they can be disastrous if you do it simply because you see other churches doing it. You don't have to make this a part of your church to be successful.

In either situation, get people to focus on church. Instill the importance of regular church attendance in your new converts with unrelenting zeal. (Hebrews 10:24,25.)

Visits or Phone Calls — Pick One

As was stated under the section, "Altar Worker Guidelines," a follow-up contact is to be in person whenever possible, but at the very least by phone, within forty-eight hours. I strongly recommend this as a means of encouragement. What could not be covered in the prayer room because of limited time can be shared in a more relaxed way and in a more soothing atmosphere.

Prayer Duty

Leader, remind your altar workers to pray for the respondents *daily,* on each and every month's schedule.

Pre-Schedule

Be aware of any special meetings your church will be having, such as crusades or revivals. Ask as far in advance as possible for volunteer workers.

Have a list in the prayer room where workers can sign up for the meetings they will attend and work. Be prepared for large responses to altar calls when guest speakers come in, especially evangelists!

Show Appreciation to Your Workers

Your workers are the ones who are really committed to your church now or are learning to commit. Be sure to show your appreciation to them for their faithfulness and diligent effort *on a continual basis.* Never let your imagination rest on coming up with ways to say, "Thank you!" Your thoughts and actions will pay great dividends.

Here are a few suggestions:

1. Have an appreciation banquet. (Your church pays.)

2. Take them out for lunch individually. (You or your church pays.)

3. Send birthday cards to them.

4. Mention them as a group from the pulpit and express thanksgiving for their work.

5. Have fellowships for groups of helps ministries separately or mix them, i.e., altar workers with ushers, children's workers with altar workers. The church should provide drinks and chips or snacks for these gatherings.

What About Children?
• • •

I am aware of the fact that some churches do not believe doctrinally that a young child can comprehend or receive salvation. I take exception to that doctrine.

My two-and-a-half-year-old son was taking a bath one day and suddenly out of him came this statement: "I want to ask Jesus into my heart, Mommy!" My wife immediately led him in a prayer to do that very thing.

I believe the same care and concern which we expend on adults should be exercised on behalf of even very young children. Perhaps because children don't respond to an altar call as dramatically as adults, we do not feel the need to work with them specifically in this area.

Bear in mind that when adults respond to an altar call they are under conviction for their sins, which can cause them to be visibly emotional. Children at an early age have not yet gone deeply into sin. Their response however, though seemingly stayed and unemotional, should not be misconstrued for an inability on their part to understand getting saved or baptized in the Holy Spirit and being able to receive.

I would encourage your church to have programs set up for children and youth that are similar to its adult program. Be sure to have good materials to hand out to *every* age group.[2]

---

[2] I highly recommend the materials that are available through Willie George Ministries. To receive a free catalog or to place an order, you may call this toll-free number: 1-800-888-7856.

Altar Work and the Law
•••

I would like to mention this subject briefly as "a word to the wise." This is a time when a spirit of lawlessness seems to be prevailing, as you are probably aware. I have heard that lawyers are actually conducting seminar classes on how to sue churches. So as the pastor it is important to cover yourself with protection. You probably have some kind of liability coverage for your church. As an example for cost and coverage comparisons, I will mention a major insurance company, Preferred Risk Group, or P.R.G.[1]

P.R.G. has in its church package a section for Counselor's Liability Insurance (CLI). In researching this material, I was reminded of just how crazy things are getting. Let me give you some examples of lawsuits levied against churches.

A lady sued a church because the pastor placed his hand on her head while praying for her healing. His touch was unsolicited.

---

[1] The Preferred Risk Group is the insurance company that pioneered church insurance coverage some forty years ago. It is a nationwide company. If you do not yet have the liability coverage you need, I recommend you get in touch with a company representative or independent agent. There is a variety of coverage that may suit your church's needs.

An evangelist, while preaching one night, saw a man in the congregation he felt it necessary to call upon. Quoting a healing Scripture, he told the man to run and he would follow. The man did as instructed. They ran around the church, up onto the platform, then down the steps. As the man came off the platform, he somehow landed in such a way that both his ankles were shattered. He sued and won.

This next example relates specifically to altar working: Two ladies prayed with and talked to a woman who had come forward in the altar call. The woman was distraught because her husband had recently left her. One of the ladies told her the Lord had said, "Everything will be all right." Several witnesses standing around heard what was said, including this woman's children. Two days later, the woman committed suicide. The children sued, and the judge awarded a large six-figure settlement to the surviving family members.

A lawyer may tell his/her clients, "Go ahead and sue. You aren't suing the church; you are suing the insurance company." This may sound like an argument against having insurance, but it is not. I believe strongly that the time period in which we live has changed drastically for the worst in this regard over the past twenty years.

Please prayerfully consider this type of insurance coverage, if you do not already have it. I believe this old saying in most every case is true: it is better to have something you don't need than something you don't have. Yes, it can be costly, but what could it save? If the church budget will not allow for the coverage, let me suggest that you at least research the subject so that when finances permit, you can, if you choose, contract with the right insurance company for you as soon as possible. The CLI

(Counselor's Liability Insurance) also allows you to include the names of staff members whom you have designated as counselors in the literal sense of the word, and they are then covered under the policy for your protection.

Now for my last quick thought about altar working and the law, you may remember, I suggested earlier in the book that you get and check references for potential workers. I also recommended oral and written exams of these workers. This is as much for your protection as it is to be used by you to determine a worker's readiness for service. Keep good records of the screening processes you use so that you may draw upon them if the need arises.

Altar Counselors — or Workers?
• • •

Notice I have not used the term *counselor* with any reference to workers you have in your altar program. This is only a small point, but one I feel is important. Give it some consideration. There are two obvious benefits:

First, it takes the idea of counselor out of the respondent's mind. If the minister says *altar workers* as opposed to *counselors,* the thought is not placed in the minds of respondents that they are being counseled in any way. Secondly, it keeps that mind-set out of your workers, and they don't think in terms of counseling.

This is not the answer for alleviating all problems from occurring, and legally it is not required, but it does make sense.

If you are just starting out in your church, do this from the beginning. If you already have "altar counselors," begin to phase out the title *counselors* and substitute *workers*. This brief chapter should emphasize the importance of training your workers well. They need to be made aware — not fearful, but aware — of the importance of sticking with the program that has been outlined to them and of staying within the parameters or boundaries set for them regarding what can and cannot be dealt with in the prayer room.

I encourage you to consider disciplining your workers. Be willing to suspend them for a time, if necessary. If you lose them as altar workers because they become offended, you may be better off.

Through proper training, and knowing those who labor among you — at least as well as possible in this kind of situation — you should pretty much know that your workers are mature enough to do their jobs competently.

Hopefully, you have not had to, nor will you ever have to, deal with circumstances relating to problems that arise from what I call the "trap of misdirected sincerity." This would be a problem created because someone steps outside their authority, for whatever reason, and causes that problem.

There are several possible causes for a worker to step outside their authority. I want to deal specifically with one of them, which is somewhat obscure from the rest. I have chosen to focus on this one because I find the others can easily fall into being intentional or wrongly motivated. The motivation for this problem creator is good, but it creates problems nonetheless and must be discussed.

"MISDIRECTED SINCERITY"
•••

I personally have shared numerous times as an altar worker. Occasionally, the people I have worked with have tried to carry the conversation in a different direction from that which would help me to accomplish my goal concerning their need. They seemed to want to talk about their past or about some problem they were dealing with at the time.

You may at some point find yourself in the same kind of situation. As I mentioned before, don't allow yourself to be sidetracked.

This section is written to help you avoid such a pitfall that could be brought about if improperly handled. Should you be faced with it, keep this in mind.

When people come forward in an altar call, their emotions are running high. They could be having all kinds of feelings, such as guilt, sorrow, shame, remorse, fear. Some people will show these feelings outwardly; others will not.

For a variety of reasons, including what was just mentioned, some people may choose at this time to open up to you about their past. Or they may have consciously decided that now would be a good time to unload their problems on someone. Seeing you as a representative of God, so to speak, they feel you are the right one to talk to about their problems, so they might be seeking counsel from you.

Also, bear in mind that as a person you have your own emotional feelings, opinions and thoughts to deal with. Your compassion and your desire to help these people may be strong at this time. Because of your feelings, you might be tempted to help them personally by giving suggestions about how they might get out of the problems and circumstances they are facing and struggling with. Your "sincere" desire to help may misdirect you into becoming a counselor instead of an altar worker.

Their problem may even be something you have faced in the past and have overcome. You might be thinking: Why shouldn't I share the answer? *After all, I'm a capable person, and it really wouldn't hurt anything!*

Or you might think: *I heard our pastor talk about the answer to this problem just last week, so I'll share what he said. We're supposed to help, aren't we?*

Perhaps you may feel a word of knowledge or word of wisdom rising up within you. If God has given this word to you, it's your responsibility to give it out, isn't it — or is it?

No, it isn't!

Ask yourself, "Would the Lord have me go beyond the authority I have been given as an altar worker?"

Your purpose as an altar worker is to minister God's Word in only three areas: salvation, restoration and the baptism in the Holy Spirit. Have you been called to a church staff position and been given an assignment from your pastor to do the counseling for your church? Unless you have, the best thing you can do is to concentrate solely on sharing about those three areas. Leave counseling to your church staff unless it is a part of your job description.

Counseling entails giving advice to people and recommending a course of action to be taken. When they are dealing with problems concerning their spiritual condition or natural circumstances beyond those three areas, it is not your place to advise them on what to do about anything. If you were to do this, you would be stepping out of your authority, even though what you have to say may be right.

When altar workers go beyond their authority and give counsel because they "simply want to help," they have moved into what I call "misdirected sincerity."

An Example of "Misdirected Sincerity"

You have probably heard the expression, "You can be sincere, but be sincerely wrong." The Bible gives us a great but tragic example of this in the book of 2 Samuel:

> Again, David gathered together all the chosen men of Israel, thirty thousand.
>
> And David arose, and went with all the people that were with him from Baale of Judah, to bring up from thence the ark of God, whose name is called by the name of the Lord of hosts that dwelleth between the cherubims.
>
> And they set [made to ride] the ark of God upon a new cart, and brought it out of the house of Abinadab that was in Gibeah: and Uzzah and Ahio, the sons of Abinadab, drave the new cart.
>
> And they brought it out of the house of Abinadab which was at Gibeah, accompanying the ark of God: and Ahio went before the ark.
>
> And David and all the house of Israel played before the Lord on all manner of instruments made of fir wood, even on harps, and on psalteries, and on timbrels, and on cornets, and on cymbals.
>
> And when they came to Nachon's threshingfloor, Uzzah put forth his hand to the ark of God, and took hold of it; for the oxen shook it.
>
> And the anger of the Lord was kindled against Uzzah; and God smote him there for his error; and there he died by the ark of God.
>
> And David was displeased, because the Lord had made a breach upon Uzzah: and he called the name of the place Perez-uzzah to this day.
>
> 2 Samuel 6:1-8

Here in Scripture we see a perfect example of "misdirected sincerity."

I define "misdirected sincerity" as: an expression in word or deed that is brought about by a sincere desire to help and be a blessing, but that brings about negative results or circumstances. Another good definition I have for it is: a wrong thing done out of a pure motive.

In the case of Uzzah whom we just read about, we trust that he was motivated by a sincere desire to keep the ark of God from falling off the cart and breaking into pieces. He was simply trying to save the ark.

Now what could be wrong with that? It was an innocent act! Besides that, the ark should not have been carried in a new cart. Uzzah should never have been put in the position of having to protect the ark from falling off the cart.

Look at what 2 Samuel 6:9 says:

And David was afraid of the Lord that day, and said, How shall the ark of the Lord come to me?

David should have asked this question before he started. He should have sought Levitical counsel before he did anything. The book of Exodus is clear on this subject. The ark had been made to be carried on staves (poles), which were to be placed through the rings on the sides of the ark by Levitical priests. (Exodus 25:10-15; Numbers 4:1,4,15.)

Another thought on this is that both David and Uzzah may have been totally ignorant of what God had said in Scripture about the ark and just did not know what they were dealing with. David had the fear of God put in him quickly as a result of this tragedy. All Uzzah was trying to do was to help. He was simply doing a good deed.

The expression, "Ignorance is no excuse for the law," may have been coined here by someone. Whether or not Uzzah was ignorant or just innocent did not change what God had said would happen.

The Reality of Absolutes

In this account God is giving us a picture of the reality of *absolutes*. The cause does not affect the consequence of breaking God's law. Nothing will change what God has said! His Word is truth; or another way to say it: His Word is reality. He set forth the truth concerning handling the ark and the consequences for mishandling it. Numbers 4:15 tells us:

> **And when Aaron and his sons have made an
> end of covering the sanctuary, and all the vessels of
> the sanctuary, as the camp is to set forward; after
> that, the sons of Kohath shall come to bear it: but
> they shall not touch any holy thing, lest they die.
> These things are the burden of the sons of Kohath
> in the tabernacle of the congregation.**

The account of Uzzah's tragic experience illustrates dramatically that what I am talking about here is extremely serious.

The Value of Submission

In some circumstances, we all have been guilty of "misdirected sincerity." Hopefully, the negative consequences were not too severe, and we learned a lesson from our actions.

To avoid this problem in the future, we must learn the value of submission. In every area of life, submission to what is right will bring us freedom.

The Law was given to us as a **schoolmaster to bring us unto Christ** (Galatians 3:24). The Law not only reveals man's inability to live up to God's standards, it also revealed God's character. If He were a man, He would not steal or murder someone or commit adultery. Jesus certainly bore out this truth.

So, as an altar worker, you may feel the pressure from your own desire to help and be a blessing to give someone advice or "a word from God." Just don't do it! Submit to the limitations placed on you by your church's guidelines.

Bear in mind, you are not the only means God has of getting people the counsel they need. You should be free to get help from a church staff member if it is an extreme situation. If, for instance, suicide is mentioned, you must report it to a staff member.

What you do in the prayer room is very important. However, it is only one of many steps forward a person must take to develop and grow in his/her personal relationship with God. I don't want to diminish its importance. I also, however, do not want to think more highly of myself as an altar worker than I ought to think.

Study to show yourself approved as an altar worker. (2 Timothy 2:15.) Learn your guidelines well. Recognize their benefit to you, as well as to your church. Never hesitate to call for assistance, instead of becoming guilty of "misdirected sincerity."

Sample Forms and Handouts
• • •

Here are the various sample forms and written works, *What About Water Baptism?* and *Your Next Steps,* all of which were referred to previously in the book.

The sample forms are made available for you, the leadership, to reprint and use in your church's helps ministry (altar worker) programs. Make any changes you deem necessary and insert the appropriate information, such as your church's name.

These forms and writings should help you to communicate what you expect from your workers and provide you with some insight into their character.

Here is an idea for the layout of the Helps Application for you to consider using. The following "application" can be designed to fit its pages on one 11" x 17" piece of paper printed on both sides. Page 1, "Qualifications For All Helps Ministries Workers"; page 2, "Confidential Helps Ministries Worker Application"; page 3, "List (name and address) of other churches you have attended regularly..."; page 4, "Indicate Areas of Interest."

(Your Church's Name)

QUALIFICATIONS FOR ALL HELPS MINISTRIES WORKERS

Christians who are in places of responsibility in our church are required to be examples in faith, conduct and business affairs. To maintain a high standard for workers is one of the best ways to present Christ to the people of our community. Therefore, the following guidelines will be required of any person who works in any of the ministries at (church's name):

1. Must be in agreement with the tenets of faith of (church's name).

2. Must be a member of (church's name) or be involved in the membership process.

3. Must be able to make a minimum six-month commitment.

4. Must complete a Helps Ministries Worker Application.

5. Must be loyal to the pastor and leaders of (church's name).

6. Must be faithful to their assigned position.

7. Must live a separated Christian life.

8. Must attend all workers' meetings and workshops.

9. Must be faithful to regular church services.

10. Must give at least three days' notice if they know they will be absent.

11. Must be at their designated post 30 minutes before starting time.

12. Must be neat in their appearance.

13. Must complete appropriate workers' training course(s) required in their area of ministry.

14. Must have their home life in order.

15. Must give 30 days' notice when resigning their position.

Please read and sign:

I have read the above qualifications and pledge to keep them to the very best of my ability. I clearly understand that failure to keep any of the above qualifications is grounds for dismissal.

_____

Signature

_____

Date

CONFIDENTIAL

(YOUR CHURCH'S NAME) HELPS MINISTRIES WORKER APPLICATION

This application is to be completed by all applicants for any position (volunteer or compensated) within (your church's name). It is being used to help the church provide a safe and secure environment for those who participate in our programs and use our facilities.

Date_____

Name _____

Address _____

City_____ State___ Zip_____ Phone(___) _____

Male/Female__ Birth Date_____ Marital Status___ No. of Children __

Spouse's name (if married)_____ Anniversary Date _____

Is your spouse involved in (your church's name) helps ministry? Yes___ No__ If yes, where?_____

Maiden Name_____ Your S.S. #('s) present and past _____

Alias (or other names you've gone by) _____

Present Employer_____

May we call you at work? _____ Work Phone (___) _____

Are you a member of (your church's name)? _____

How long have you attended (your church's name)? _____

Have you been born again?___ If yes, where?_____ Year _____

Have you been filled with the Holy Spirit according to Acts 2:4? _____

If yes, where?_____ Year _____

Have you been baptized in water?_____ If yes, where? _____

Do you tithe on a regular basis to (your church's name)? _____

DO YOU BELIEVE:

YES   NO

____ ____ In the Virgin Birth and the deity of our Lord Jesus Christ?

____ ____ That Jesus is God's Son and the only sacrifice for sin?

____ ____ That man must be born again to receive eternal life?

____ ____ In eternal reward for the believer (heaven)?

____ ____ In eternal damnation for the lost (hell)?

____ ____ In the Rapture of the Church prior to the seven-year tribulation?

____ ____ In the infallibility of the Scriptures?

____ ____ That divine healing is part of redemption's purchase and is God's will for all who believe?

____ ____ That Jesus rose bodily from the dead?

____ ____ In the infilling of the Holy Spirit?

____ ____ That speaking in tongues is the initial physical evidence of the baptism in the Holy Spirit?

List (name and address) of other churches you have attended regularly during the past five years: _____

_____

_____

List any gifts, callings, training, education or other factors that have prepared you for Christian service: _____

_____

_____

Have you ever led anyone to Christ? ___Yes ___No

Have you ever helped anyone receive the Holy Spirit? ___Yes ___No

Have you ever been involved in helps ministries before? ___Yes ___No

If yes, in what areas? _____

_____

With what church or organization? _____

Do you have any physical handicaps or conditions preventing you from performing certain types of activities relating to helps ministries? ___Yes ___No

If yes, please explain: _____

_____

Have you been accused of and/or convicted of child abuse or a crime involving actual or attempted sexual molestation of a minor? ___Yes ___No

If yes, please explain: _____

_____

Have you been involved in homosexual activity within the last five years? ___Yes ___No

Do you presently have any communicable diseases (including HIV or AIDS)? ___Yes ___No

If yes, please explain: _____

_____

Do you smoke? _____ Drink? _____ Use illegal drugs? _____

Why do you want to be involved in the helps ministries?_____

_____

_____

INDICATE AREAS OF INTEREST

___ Altar Worker	___ Musician	___ Nursery (birth to 2)
___ Audio	___ Senior Outreach	___ Pre-School (2-6)
___ Bookstore	Ministry	___ Children's (Gr. 1-3)
___ Bus Driver	___ Prison Ministry	___ Children's (Gr. 4-6)
___ Good Samaritans	___ Safety/Traffic	___ Bus Ministry
___ Greeter	___ Singer	___ Jr. High Ministry
___ Hospital Ministry	___ Usher	___ Youth Ministry
___ Hospitality	___ Visitation Ministry	___ _____
	___ _____	

Which weekend service(s) do you normally attend?
___Saturday ___Sunday 1st ___Sunday 2nd

Which service(s) would you be able to work in?
___Saturday ___Sunday 1st ___Sunday 2nd ___Wednesday ___Bus Ministry

Is your spouse and/or family in agreement with you working in (your church's name) helps ministry?_____

PERSONAL REFERENCES
(Not employees or relatives)

Name_____Name _____
Address _____Address _____
Telephone _____Telephone _____

PASTORAL REFERENCE
(Former Senior Pastor, Associate Pastor or Ministerial Supervisor)

Name_____
Address _____
Telephone _____

APPLICANT'S STATEMENT

The information contained in this application is correct to the best of my knowledge. I authorize any references or churches listed in this application to give you any information they may have regarding my character and fitness for helps ministries. I release all such references from liability for any damage that may result from furnishing such evaluations to you, and I waive any right that I have to inspect the references provided on my behalf.

Should my application be accepted, I agree to be bound by the constitution and by-laws and policies of (your church's name) and to refrain from unscriptural conduct.

_____ _____

Applicant's Signature   Date

_____ _____

Witness' Signature   Date

(Your Church's Name)

AUTHORIZATION FOR RELEASE OF INFORMATION

In connection with my application for volunteer service with (your church's name), I authorize (your church's name) and/or ACCUFAX Div., Southwest Inc., their agent, to solicit background information relative to my criminal record history. I understand that (your church's name) may conduct inquiries into my background that may include criminal records, personal references and other public record reports pertaining to me.

I authorize without reservation, any person, agency or other entity contacted by (your church's name), or ACCUFAX Div., Southwest Inc., their agent, for purposes of obtaining background report information, to furnish the above-mentioned information.

I release (your church's name), their respective employees, or ACCUFAX Div., Southwest Inc., their agent, and employees and all persons, agencies and entities providing information or reports about me from any and all liability arising out of furnishing any such information or reports.

Please Print

Last Name_____ First Name _____

Date of Birth_____

City of Birth_____ County_____ State_____

AKA or Maiden Name_____ Social Security No._____

(Please note: if your address is a rural route or post office box, we must have the city and county your mail is delivered to.)

Current Address_____ How long at this address? ___
                                                   (months, years)

City_____ County_____ State____ Zip _____

Previous Address_____ How long at this address? ___
                                                   (months, years)

City_____ County_____ State_____ Zip _____

Signature_____ Date_____

Thank you for applying to help
in the Helps Ministries of (your church's name)

Please return this form with your Helps Ministries Application
to the Information Booth in the foyer or give it directly
to the appropriate minister or coordinator.

IMPORTANT:

- Notice that the name of "Accufax Div., Southvest Inc." has been given on the form. This is the name of the company used by Church on the Move in Tulsa, Oklahoma (as of 8/97). I suggest you find a company in your local area to do this research for your church.

- This is only an example for you to use in drafting a form of your own. This example form was drafted by an attorney in the state of Oklahoma. *It may not meet the legal qualifications in your state for its intended purpose.* Contact your church's attorney to make sure your form is appropriate and complies with all the laws in your state for requesting information of this nature.

FOLLOW-UP REPORT

The sample Follow-up Report asks for information beyond the name, address and phone number of respondents and why they answered the altar call. Please have them fill out the form completely. All the information they provide will greatly help in efforts to follow up on those ministered to in the prayer room.

The Follow-up Report form should be printed on two-copy or three-copy NCR paper. If your church does not use this type of form, you should make up the kind of report that will allow you to properly follow up on the respondents, as well as to provide all necessary staff members a copy for their records.

SAMPLE FOLLOW-UP REPORT

Last Name	First Name

Address	Phone

City	State	Zip

Birth Date   Marital Status

___Male ___Female ___/___/___

Reason for coming:

___Salvation ___Restoration ___Baptism of Holy Spirit ___Other

Have you been water baptized?   ___Yes   ___No

Are you a member of a church?   ___Yes   ___No

If so, what is the name of the church?

What is the best time to contact you?   a.m.   p.m.

Phone number or address where you may be contacted: (If different from above)

Prayer Room Worker's Information

Prayer Room Worker's Name	Date

Remarks:

___Received well ___Received with hesitation ___Had questions

___Did not receive ___Other (please explain): _____

Comments on follow-up:	Date of follow-up

White - Prayer Room Worker; Canary - Prayer Coordinator;

Pink - Pastoral Staff

ALTAR WORKER AVAILABILITY REPORT

	WEEK 1	WEEK 2	WEEK 3	WEEK 4	WEEK 5
SATURDAY EVENING					
7:00 p.m.	_____	_____	_____	_____	_____
SUNDAY MORNING					
9:00 a.m.	_____	_____	_____	_____	_____
11:00 a.m.	_____	_____	_____	_____	_____
WEDNESDAY EVENING					
7:00 p.m.	_____	_____	_____	_____	_____

INSTRUCTIONS:

Please place a check mark by the week and service times for which you will be available. Remember that some months have a fifth Sunday, Wednesday or Saturday. You will fill out this form only once. This information will be placed on a master schedule, which will be used each month to schedule you according to your availability.

NAME _____

ADDRESS _____

CITY/STATE/ZIP _____

PHONE (___) _____

Please Note:

Some leaders prefer to schedule their workers as they need them rather than according to their availability. In some cases, you may have to do this in order to meet the altar-working needs of your church. If you do this, simply list your services with one line after them, as shown below:

Sunday Morning:_____

Sunday Evening: _____

Wednesday Evening: _____

(YOUR CHURCH'S NAME) ALTAR WORKER MASTER SCHEDULE

WEEK 1		WEEK 2		WEEK 3		WEEK 4		WEEK 5	
MEN	WOMEN	MEN	WOMEN	MEN	WOMEN	MEN	WOMEN	MEN	WOMEN

(List all workers
in appropriate
columns from
information
provided on
"Availability
Reports.")

Wed. Evening   Sun. Evening   Sun. Morning

SAMPLE MONTHLY ALTAR WORKER SCHEDULE

DATE	9 a.m. MEN	9 a.m. WOMEN	11 a.m. MEN	11 a.m. WOMEN
SUN 9/1	Scott E	Jeanne E	Mark A	Maralee H
	Dennis C	Victoria B	Jon R	LaDonna F
	David C	JoAnn D	John R	Jerry Ann R
	Doug B	Lorrie M	Gary K	Judy S
		Marcia C	Dan M	Mary B
WED 9/4	David C	Liza M		
	John M	Sherrie O		
	Russ A	Lauren M		
SUN 9/8	Doug B	Sherrie O	Rod L	Judy S
	David C	Kristen S	Paul M	Lauren M
	Dennis C	Marcia C	John M	LaDonna F
	Scott E	Darlene L	Greg S	Helen E
		Ann C	Bill H	Maralee H
WED 9/11	Greg S	Darlene L		
	Kevin M	Liza M		
	Scott E	Lorrie M		
SUN 9/15	Charles T	Kathy C	Gary K	Jerry Ann R
	Doug B	Liza M	John R	Jessie H
	Scott E	Sherrie O	John M	Linda H
	Russ A	Darlene L	Henry H	LaDonna F
		Debbie T	Jon R	Lauren M
WED 9/18	Kevin M	Kristen S		
	Russ A	Maralee H		
	Greg S	Kathy C		
SUN 9/22	David C	Lorrie M	Dan M	Linda H
	Doug B	Darlene L	Bill H	Mary B
	Kevin M	Kathy C	Mark A	Maralee H
	Dennis C	Sherrie O	Paul M	Judy S
	Russ A	Liza M	Rod L	Linda M
WED 9/25	John M	Marcia C		
	Scott E	Darlene L		
	Kevin M	Lauren M		
SUN 9/29	Dennis C	Marcia C	Jon R	Lauren M
	Scott E	Lorrie M	Mark A	Linda H
	David C	Darlene L	Gary K	Linda M
	Russ A	Liza M	Dan M	Jerry Ann R
		Kathy C	John M	Judy S

Thank you all for your faithfulness! I have switched couples around on purpose in order to make it easier for follow-up visits.

Please join us at the Couples' Fellowships if you can. We will still have Altar Workers Fellowships on a regular basis, once every three months or so.

(YOUR CHURCH'S NAME)
ALTAR WORKER RECORD SHEET 19___

My little children, of whom I travail in birth again until Christ be formed in you — Galatians 4:19

PLEASE PRAY EPHESIANS 1:17-19 AND 3:16-21 FOR THESE PEOPLE DAILY!

NAME	ADDRESS	PHONE	REASON FOR RESPONSE	WATER BAPTISM YES/NO
FOLLOW-UP COMMENTS		CONTINUE ON BACK		DATE OF CONTACT

(YOUR CHURCH'S NAME)
ALTAR WORKER RECORD SHEET
INSTRUCTIONS

1) Fill in information from (your church's name) Follow-Up Report.

2) Record comments from initial visit (made within 48 hours of their response to the altar) on line 1 of the "Comments" section. Additional comments may be recorded below.

3) Record date of contact.

4) On line 2 of "Comments" section, record comments from second follow-up (phone call) made within 7-10 days after your first visit. If they have no phone, either drop by for a visit (leaving a note if they are not in) or write a letter to them, keeping your initial visit in mind. Please record in the "Comments" section that a letter was sent or that you left a note when you tried to visit them.

5) Record date of second contact.

THIS SHEET IS TO BE RETURNED TO PRAYER ROOM
OR HEAD ALTAR WORKER UPON COMPLETION.

PERSON NUMBER	VISIT NUMBER 1 OR 2	FOLLOW-UP COMMENTS	CONTINUED FROM FRONT SIDE

WHAT ABOUT WATER BAPTISM?

The following is a handout on water baptism for those to whom you minister. If you desire, you may develop your own pamphlet using this as the text.

ANSWERS TO QUESTIONS ABOUT WATER BAPTISM
FROM GOD'S WORD
• • •

Why Should I Be Baptized?

> Go ye into all the world, and preach the gospel to every creature.
>
> He that believeth and is baptized shall be saved; but he that believeth not shall be damned.
>
> Mark 16:15,16

> And Jesus came and spake unto them, saying, All power is given unto me in heaven and in earth.
>
> Go ye therefore, and teach all nations, baptizing them in the name of the Father, and of the Son, and of the Holy Ghost:
>
> Teaching them to observe all things whatsoever I have commanded you: and, lo, I am with you alway, even unto the end of the world. Amen.
>
> Matthew 28:18-20

These verses from the Bible tell us of Jesus' last instructions to His disciples before He ascended into heaven. I have found it to be true that last instructions are often some of the most important ones a person will communicate to us.

If you look at water baptism this way, I think you will realize how important it is to follow Jesus in it.

Then cometh Jesus from Galilee to Jordan
unto John, to be baptized of him.

But John forbad him, saying, I have need to be
baptized of thee, and comest thou to me?

And Jesus answering said unto him, Suffer it
to be so now: for thus it becometh us to fulfil all
righteousness. Then he suffered him.

Matthew 3:13-15

Being water baptized should be done by you in
obedience to God's Word. The act itself is an outward sign of
an inward grace in your life. By having your entire physical
body lowered into the water, you are showing outwardly to
other believers, as well as to the world, that you have made
the decision to follow Jesus with your whole life.

The subject of water baptism is also spoken of in the
book of Romans, chapter 6. The apostle Paul writes:

Know ye not, that so many of us as were
baptized into Jesus Christ were baptized into
his death?

Therefore we are buried with him by baptism
into death: that like as Christ was raised up from
the dead by the glory of the Father, even so we also
should walk in newness of life.

Romans 6:3,4

Water baptism is a living picture you can paint in your
life of what Jesus did in His death, burial and resurrection.
After having been baptized, you will, in a sense, be able to
relate to what He has done for you by having symbolically
done it yourself.

The like figure whereunto even baptism doth
also now save us (not the putting away of the filth

of the flesh, but the answer of a good conscience toward God,) by the resurrection of Jesus Christ.

1 Peter 3:21

How Should I Be Baptized?

The Bible must be our guide. Notice particularly the following Scripture verses, with italics added for emphasis:

And Jesus, when he was baptized, *went up straightway out of the water*: and, lo, the heavens were opened unto him, and he saw the Spirit of God descending like a dove, and lighting upon him.

Matthew 3:16

And he commanded the chariot to stand still: and *they went down both into the water*, both Philip and the eunuch; and he baptized him.

And *when they were come up out of the water*, the Spirit of the Lord caught away Philip....

Acts 8:38,39

Therefore we are *buried* with him by baptism into death....

Romans 6:4

Webster's dictionary defines *bury* as "to hide or cover." Only immersion fulfills this definition. Also, the Greek word used here for baptism is *baptizo*, which means "to make whelmed (i.e., fully wet)."[1] So, that means you need to be fully immersed.

---

[1] James H. Strong. *Strong's Exhaustive Concordance.* Compact Ed. (Grand Rapids: Baker, 1992), "Greek Dictionary of the New Testament," p. 18, #907.

In What Name Should I Be Baptized?

We find this question clearly answered by God's Word in Matthew 28:19. In this Scripture verse Jesus says:

> Go ye therefore, and teach all nations, baptizing them in the name of the Father, and of the Son, and of the Holy Ghost.

When Should I Be Baptized?

Again, we must go to God's Word for the answer. (Italics are added for emphasis.)

> But *when they believed* Philip preaching the things concerning the kingdom of God, and the name of Jesus Christ, they were baptized, both men and women.
>
> Then Simon himself believed also: and when he was baptized, he continued with Philip....
>
> Then Philip opened his mouth, and began at the same scripture, and *preached unto him Jesus.*
>
> And *as they went on their way, they came unto a certain water:* and the eunuch said, See, here is water; what doth hinder me to be baptized? And *Philip said, If thou believest with all thine heart, thou mayest.* And he answered and said, I believe that Jesus Christ is the Son of God.
>
> And he commanded the chariot to stand still: and *they went down both into the water, both Philip and the eunuch; and he baptized him.*
>
> Acts 8:12,13,35-38

> And they spake unto him the word of the Lord, and to all that were in his house.

And he took them *the same hour of the night,*
and washed their stripes; *and was baptized, he and*
all his, straightway [without delay].

Acts 16:32,33

You should be water baptized as soon as you can after
you have been saved. Don't put it off. If you have been saved
for some time — whether one year, twenty years, or even
more — and have not yet been baptized, you still need to
follow the Lord's command in this. Remember, His instructions to you have not changed. We will be blessed to see you
follow the Lord's instruction, no matter how long it has been
since you received salvation.

I hope this teaching will be helpful to you in deciding to
be baptized. Your quick obedience will bless you greatly in
your walk with God.

INSTRUCTIONS TO CANDIDATE FOR BAPTISM
...

Leaders, feel free to change the following instructions to suit
your own church's program.

Water baptism services are held once a month at (your
church's name), usually on the second Sunday during the
11:00 A.M. service. (Be sure to check your bulletin for any
schedule changes.) Please sign up for water baptism at the
Information Booth and follow the guidelines given below to
prepare for the water baptism service:

1. Meet in the Prayer Room no later than 11:00 A.M. for
   instructions.

2. Come wearing the clothes in which you will be baptized.

3. Wear dark-colored clothing that covers your whole body.

4. Wear a full set of undergarments.

5. Be sure to bring a change of clothes, including under-garments, and some kind of container to hold your wet clothes.

6. Bring a towel and other personal items (i.e., hair dryer, makeup) for use after baptism.

Any baptismal candidate who does not follow these instructions will be asked to wait until the next baptism service.

Insert Name and Address
of Your Church
Here

YOUR NEXT STEPS
WHAT DO YOU DO FROM NOW ON?
• • •

This pamphlet will tell you what God wants you to do now that you have been born again spiritually. You are in control of how rapidly you grow in your understanding of what has happened to you and in your knowledge of God Himself.

The Holy Spirit inspired the apostle Peter to speak directly to you in the New Testament book of 1 Peter, chapter 2, verses 2 and 3:

> **As newborn babes, *desire* the sincere milk of the word, that ye may *grow* thereby** (italics added for emphasis):
>
> **If so be ye have tasted that the Lord is gracious.**

NOW THAT YOU ARE SAVED
• • •

What a wonderful thing you have done. No person alive has a more important and crucial decision to make than to accept or reject faith in Jesus. You have chosen wisely to receive the truth you heard from the book of Romans, chapter 10, verses 9 and 10. In *The New King James Version*[2] of the Bible, this passage of Scripture says:

> **...if you confess with your mouth the Lord Jesus and believe in your heart that God has raised Him [Jesus] from the dead, you will be saved.**
>
> **For with the heart one believes unto righteousness, and with the mouth confession is made unto salvation.**

---

[2] (Nashville: Thomas Nelson, 1988), p. 997.

The moment you prayed that prayer from your heart (from down inside), you were changed by the Holy Spirit. Right then, He made you a new creature. Spiritually, you are now a child of God because you have been born again. You are a new member of the family of God.

As your brothers and sisters in Christ, we are thrilled for you! We hope someday perhaps you will join us as a member of (church's name) and make this your church home.

But Now What?
· · ·

At this point you might be wondering: *Where do I go from here?*

We will start by asking you to consider the following situation:

Imagine you are suddenly kidnapped by a foreign government agency, taken to its country and told in no uncertain terms that you can never leave there and return to your own country. What would you do then?

You are given a book telling of the customs, economy, society and language of that country to help you, then are told to fend for yourself. What will you do to survive in that strange land? Think about it for a moment.

The people are different. Their customs and behavior are strange to you. The laws governing them are unique. They have a different economic system than you have ever known. And of course, their language is completely foreign to you. What a challenge you would face.

There would be so much for you to learn to answer all the questions you would have in order to survive! You would have to learn that new language to be able to communicate. You would need to get a job and make money for food and shelter. And all you were given was a book to teach you.

How valuable would that book be to you? How much effort would you put into reading and studying it?

Remember, you would never be allowed to return to your home country and you would be living out the rest of your life in that new country.

In the New Testament book of Colossians, chapter 1, verse 13 it tells us that God **hath delivered us** (that's you) **from the power** (or kingdom) **of darkness, and hath translated us into** (or placed you in) **the kingdom of his dear Son.**

Welcome to the new country! As a believer in Jesus Christ, you are now living in a new place "spiritually." You have been given a book that will teach you about the kingdom of God in which you now live. (Read *The New Birth*, which was included in your packet.)

Keeping in mind our questions to you as we go, let's talk briefly about what you need to do.

A GIFT AFTER SALVATION
• • •

We will start with good news: there is a second gift after salvation, which God (the Father, Son and Holy Spirit) wants you to have. It is the power to be a witness for Jesus (an example in words and actions) to your family, friends and acquaintances.

The New Testament book of Acts, chapter 1, verse 8, says:

> But ye shall receive power, after that the Holy
> Ghost is come upon you: and ye shall be witnesses
> unto me both in Jerusalem, and in all Judaea, and in
> Samaria, and unto the uttermost part of the earth.

Jesus wanted His disciples to wait for this power to come on them before they started sharing the good news about Him to the world. They were already born again, just like you are, but they needed to receive this *second* gift from God to help them fulfill His plan for their lives. You do too!

At the same time you receive that power, God will give you a new tongue (or spiritual language) for you to use in praying to God along with the language you speak now.

In the New Testament book of Acts, chapter 2, verses 38 and 39, it says this is promised to all who would become believers.

Jesus commanded the disciples to wait until they had received it before going into the world to preach the Gospel (Acts 1:4,5,8).

According to the gospel of Mark in the New Testament, certain things go along with being a believer. One of these things is found in Mark, chapter 16, verse 17, where Jesus says, **They shall speak with new tongues.**

All you need do to receive a new tongue is to ask for it in prayer. This new language is understood by God, but not by us without His help, because it is on a spiritual level. The Holy Spirit is giving you the words (utterance) to speak out loud with your mouth. Pray and ask God to fill you with the Holy Spirit, that you be given the power you need and a new spiritual language to live in the kingdom of God. In the packet you have been given a copy of *Why Tongues?* to help you understand more about this subject.

GET BAPTIZED!
• • •

Now that you are saved, the Lord wants you to follow Him in water baptism. As was pointed out earlier in our study, the word *baptism* literally means being immersed. It is important for you to know that nothing you do in your flesh can save you, like getting baptized for instance. As it says in the New Testament book of Ephesians, it is your faith that saves you.

> **For by grace are ye saved *through faith*; and that not of yourselves: it is the gift of God** (italics added for emphasis):
>
> **Not of works, lest any man should boast.**
>
> **Ephesians 2:8,9**

Jesus, however, told His disciples to go into all the world and preach the Gospel (the Good News) to everyone, baptizing them in the name of the Father and the Son and the Holy Spirit. (Matthew 28:19.) We encourage you to obey the Lord in this soon by being baptized at this church or another one near you.

GOD'S COVENANT BOOK
• • •

Now let's talk about the Book that God has given us: the Bible. Its purpose is to help us learn how to survive in the present world in which we are living physically and in the new place where we are spiritually *as God's children.*

The Bible contains the most important words ever written. Have you ever heard someone say, "I got inspired to do this or that"? Well, the writers of the books in the Bible were inspired by God to write the words He told them, and they did.

Simply put, the Bible includes two sets of books, the Old Testament and the New Testament, that were combined into one to reveal God and His plan and purpose for His creation, of which you are a part.

God made a covenant with mankind. This was a sworn agreement, sealed in the shed blood of Jesus. It is impossible for God to free Himself or to change in any way. If we will do as He has instructed, He will do what He has said. In other words, you do your part; God will always do His part.

The Old Testament (Old Covenant) is a revelation of how God worked in people's lives before He could send His Son Jesus to make salvation possible. Then after Jesus came, died on the Cross and was resurrected, God sent the Holy Spirit to reveal how He now works with us in our lives. This is the New Testament (New Covenant).

As was pointed out earlier, if you suddenly found yourself in that new and strange land, wouldn't you cherish the book you had been given? After all, it would be your lifeline to survival.

Well, God's Word — the Bible — should be just as important to you. The words in the Bible were inspired by Almighty God. The Holy Spirit spoke to men in their heart, and they wrote down what they heard.

FEED ON GOD'S WORD
...

We strongly encourage you to read the Bible daily. Start in the New Testament. Read the gospel of John first; then go to the other books. The New Testament epistles, or letters, are very important, because they really explain how you are to live and behave in the kingdom of God.

Another reason God wants you to read His Word daily is because it will help you to become tuned in to the sound of His voice. God wants to speak to you! He does it in various ways:

1. Through His Word

2. Down in your heart (see Proverbs 20:27 and John 10:27)

3. Through ministers of the Gospel

4. Sometimes through other believers.

In the gospel of John, Jesus said:

> **If ye abide in me, and my words abide in you** (in other words, if they continue to be read and thought upon as you go about your daily affairs), **ye shall ask what ye will, and it shall be done unto you.**
>
> **John 15:7**

> **If ye continue in my word** (to read it consistently and think about it as you go about your daily affairs), **then are ye my disciples indeed;**
>
> **And ye shall know the truth** (reality in both the physical world and the spiritual world), **and** (knowing) **the truth** (reality) **shall make you free.**
>
> **John 8:31,32**

Here Jesus tells us that the Bible, or His words, will reveal the "why" of things in this world — *if we choose to continue reading and thinking about it from now on!* It will also tell us about the spiritual realm which, though invisible to our eyes, is a major part of the reality in which we live! We cannot truly understand the Truth, or reality, until we begin to understand both the physical and spiritual parts of our existence. Gaining this understanding is a growing process that has just begun for you, and one that will take time.

In order to grow and survive, you feed your body three times a day, so you need to feed your spirit the words of God. Jesus said, **The words that I speak unto you, they are spirit, and they are life** (John 6:63). As a believer, you need to live by *every* word that proceeds from the mouth of God (Matthew 4:4).

LEARN TO HEAR GOD'S VOICE
•••

Yes, you can learn to hear God's voice. He will sound the same as the voice you "hear" when you are reading His Word.

Always remember: what you hear, no matter who the source may be, should never disagree with what is written in the Bible. Consider tuning out some of the voices you hear constantly through TV, radio and newspapers so that you will become familiar with the sound of God's voice.

LEARN TO READ BIBLE REFERENCES
•••

The materials we have given you in the packet are loaded with references (or referrals) to different Scripture verses in the Bible. We will use two Scripture references as examples:

Mal 3:8-12, I John 1:9

The abbreviation you see here is telling you which of the 66 different books of the Bible is being referred to. First, look in the index of your Bible and check for an abbreviation list or table of contents to find the book that begins with the letters "Mal." As you will see, this stands for the Old Testament book of *Malachi*.

The second example referring to a book of the Bible which includes a Roman numeral could be found in either the Old Testament or the New. In this case, a book of the Bible named John can be found only in the New Testament. Notice there are four books entitled "John." Three have Roman numerals in front of them. So this second example is referring to the book of I John.

After the name of the book is located, the number before the colon tells you the chapter of the book; the number(s) after the colon tells you the verse(s) in that chapter. The two examples we are using could be read as follows:

Mal (chapter) 3: (verses) 8 (through) 12
I John (chapter) 1: (verse) 9

COMMUNICATE WITH GOD
...

You have been translated out of Satan's kingdom and have been transferred into God's kingdom spiritually. You now have a relationship with God. This is the most important relationship you will ever have. Good, constant communication is a building block in any relationship, and that certainly applies to your relationship with God.

The Lord wants you to pray and converse with (talk to) Him daily about your life and the lives of others in relation to Him. For instance, ask Him to help you understand the Bible as you read it and think about (ponder) what it says. Pray Bible verses to God by changing the tense to first person. For example, change Ephesians 1:17,18 to read:

That the God of our Lord Jesus Christ, the Father of glory, may give unto me the spirit of wisdom and revelation in the knowledge of Him: the eyes of my understanding being enlightened; that I may know the hope of His calling and the riches of the glory of His inheritance in the saints.

Here are other passages of Scripture we recommend you look up and pray:

Ephesians 1:16-22
Ephesians 3:14-21
Colossians 1:9-14

As you read these verses and pray them, you will notice "giving thanks" is mentioned. Giving thanks to God is a part of praising or worshiping Him. You can praise God out loud or quietly inside yourself anytime, day or night. You can sing songs to Him that you have heard in church or make them up yourself. You can thank Him by just talking to Him and saying, "Thank You, Lord, for what You have done for me." You have much to be thankful for, even if you are experiencing difficult circumstances in life. You can thank God for sending Jesus and for saving you from spending eternity separate from Him in hell. You will find many more reasons to **cease not to give thanks** (Ephesians 1:16). God deserves and is worthy of your thanks and praise.

You also should pray every day in your new spiritual language — in tongues (see 1 Corinthians 14:15). You can pray in your spiritual language out loud or quietly within yourself anytime, day or night, because you control it, just like you control praying with your understanding in your own language.

Don't fail to communicate with God daily in all three ways in prayer, in praise and worship, in tongues. Shut off the TV for a while and spend some time with your new heavenly Father.

A NEW FAMILY
...

Here is some good news: unlike the person described earlier who was sent into a *strange* place, you now have a new family, the Church. Not just those who attend (your church's name) but everyone who has received Jesus as their Lord and Savior by faith just like you.

We encourage you to get to know some of us. You may find that some of your old friends may not understand or agree with the decision you have made, but you have a new family now with whom to develop relationships.

The Lord knows you have need of social interaction (friends). That's a part of why He wants you to attend church regularly. But there is another important reason for attending church regularly. It has to do with the pastor of the church you have chosen to make your home. The Lord says your pastor is a gift to you. (Ephesians 4:8,11,12.) God uses your pastor to impart to you an understanding of the way the kingdom of God works and how you are to live in it and still function in your daily life on earth.

We at (your church's name) would love for you to make this your home. Of course, if you don't live in this area, we encourage you to find a church that you can attend regularly. This is most important. Read Hebrews 10:24,25.

Our service times are: (List your service times)

Saturday	7:00 P.M.
Sunday	9:00 A.M. and 11:00 A.M.
Wednesday	7:00 P.M.

Attending church regularly will provide you with the opportunity to meet and get to know some of your brothers and sisters in Christ. This is vital to your spiritual growth. Be there!

(Your church's name) feels strongly about water baptism. A pamphlet telling you the importance of it is in your packet. Please take the time to read it. We trust you will obey the Lord's command concerning this.

LIVING A NEW LIFE IN A NEW KINGDOM
• • •

One of the biggest problems in society today is a general lack of purpose in people's lives. If you were to find yourself in the strange situation presented at the beginning of this pamphlet, your purpose would be plain: to survive in that new country, that new kingdom. You would study your book diligently, working hard at it, because your survival depended upon it.

In a sense, you are at that place now. You need to put forth some effort in learning about God and His kingdom; after all, you will be spending eternity with Him. The truth is, compared to eternity, your life here on earth is less — much less — than the blink of an eye.

Actually, when you were born again, God took care of answering questions for you like, What's my purpose? Why am I here? What's life all about? God created mankind for the purpose of establishing a relationship with each and every person who has ever lived.

So knowing God, your Creator, personally is one of the purposes you have. Then as you learn of God and how good God is, you will naturally share Him with others as a living witness (an example in words and actions) of God's love to the world through Jesus. The Bible tells us in John 3:36:

> **He that believeth on the Son** (of God) **hath everlasting life: and he that believeth not the Son shall not see life; but the wrath of God abideth on him.**

Not believing on Jesus or rejecting Him from your heart, which isn't easy to do, are the only two things that can separate someone from God and cost that person eternity without Him.

You can fulfill this purpose by diligently doing what we have shared with you in this pamphlet. And doing it consistently!

It's important for you to share Jesus. And you don't have to wait a year, a month or even a week from now to do it. Just tell your family and friends about what Jesus has done for you and that Jesus loves them too. Then invite them to church. You don't have to answer every question they may have. Church can help win your family, friends and acquaintances. So be bold! Bring them to church with you. There is nothing greater than to see someone you know come to the Lord.

GOD'S ECONOMIC SYSTEM
...

In the situation presented to you in the beginning, we said you would have to survive in that new country on your own, but that a good, basic understanding of its economy would be talked about in the book you were given.

God's kingdom also has an economic system. It's based on the fact that God wants to bless you financially so much so that you have your needs met and also that you can contribute to His work on the earth.

The financial system of this world in which we live is set up so that as much money as possible flows *away* from any church, minister or organization doing the work of God by sharing the good news about Jesus and salvation through faith in Him. In God's kingdom, money is a tool used to bless you and others through you as you give to those who are sharing God's Word.

There is something God requires of you. Read Malachi 3:8-12. God asks you to give Him the tithe, which is 10 percent of your income. The word *tithe* means "tenth."[3] It takes money to pay for spreading the Gospel. It takes money to keep a church building warm or cool and the lights on. I think you get the picture.

Tithing is something you do by faith. Faith is simply believing what you read in the Bible (belief) and doing it (action). In Malachi 3:8-10 the Lord asks you to give the tithe (tenth), or 10 percent of your earnings, to Him. If you truly believe He is asking you to give 10 percent of your income (belief), then *you will do it* (action). You exercised *faith* when you received Jesus as your Lord and Savior. You believed what the Bible said, then acted on that belief by praying a prayer. It takes the process of exercising faith (belief and corresponding action on those beliefs) to please God. (Hebrews 11:6.)

---

[3] Strong. "Hebrews and Chaldee Dictionary," p. 70, #4643.

God commands and expects you to tithe. He leaves any additional giving up to you. Keep in mind that giving 10 percent leaves you with 90 percent. We can assure you that you will have more by obeying God and being a faithful and consistent tither than if you keep all your income. God is requesting this because it gives Him the legal right to move on your behalf financially. Perhaps you will be offered overtime on your job; maybe you will find a better job; or you might get an idea from God that could turn into a money-making venture for you.

Know this, in some way God is going to bless you with something that will in turn help you financially. He says we are to prove Him, or test Him out, only about this one subject. He will prove Himself on this, whether you are struggling or doing well financially. He is asking you to trust Him in this and to be obedient as well.

You might ask, *Where do I tithe?*

The tithe (10 percent) should go to the local church you are attending. An offering, which is where giving to God really begins, is any money you give over and above your tithe. You will learn much more about this as you continue to grow and increase in your understanding of God's kingdom.

Here are two simple statements for you to learn and to remember: It is impossible for you to give more than God; and, he who gives his heart will not deny his money. I have used the analogy of being transported to a foreign country to live; given only a book to learn its customs, economy, society structure and language; to explain the basics of what God expects of you now and in the future. Now we will move in a little different direction by addressing the problem of sin.

THE PROBLEM OF SIN

...

Sin defined biblically is the transgression of the Law. Another way to think about it would be that sin is whatever God says it is, not what we want it to be or not be.

There are some things that to you are obviously sinful and wrong. As you are diligent in studying the Bible, other things will show up in your life that you may be unaware of at this time that really are sinful. If you sin, you will find that you don't feel good or at peace on the inside. The inward man (your spirit) is telling you that you are doing wrong. Learn to listen to that and stop where you are before actually doing what you know inside that you shouldn't do.

It is not, for example, a sin to have a thought such as this: "To get out of trouble, I will just lie a little bit to my boss about that." It becomes sin as you continue to think about and talk about doing that, then end up doing it. (See James 1:13-15.)

Learn to listen for that Voice that sounds the same as the Word of God when you read it. Then obey as the Holy Spirit leads you!

If you do something wrong and know you have sinned, you don't need to get saved again. First John 1:9 tells us what to do. It tells us to confess our sins to Him in prayer. God's character is spoken of here, and we are given instructions on what to do if we sin. God is faithful. He will never let you down. You may miss it, but He never will. God is just. He has the legal right to forgive you because you have exercised faith in Jesus' lordship and resurrection.

You are never justified in sin, so be good to yourself and stop sinning as He shows you the things you need to stop thinking and saying and doing. If He tells you to stop doing something or to start doing something else, it is totally for your good.

Sin is selfishness. It is deceitful. There is a high price to pay for allowing yourself to do it. The Lord says for you to be holy as He is holy. So let God define what is sinful in your life, then let Him help you remove it from your life.

BE FAITHFUL — GROW IN THE LORD!
...

Now that you are in God's kingdom, you need to do these things faithfully from now on:

- Read and study God's Word, the Bible, every day.
- Pray with your understanding and in tongues every day.
- Praise and worship God every day.
- Attend church regularly.
- Share Jesus with those around you and invite them to church.
- Tithe (give 10 percent of your income) to the church you regularly attend.
- Be willing to let certain behaviors and thoughts go out of your life as God shows you what they are. Let *Him* define sin for you; then *you* stop it.

If you will do these things faithfully, you will quickly grow in your understanding of the Truth (reality).

We have given you other materials which were selected by our pastor to help you grow in the Lord. Please read and study them. They will bless you and help you to know God and His purpose for your life.

This is only the beginning of your new life in God's kingdom. May God bless you!

Submit yourselves therefore to God. Resist the devil, and he will flee from you.

Draw nigh to God, and he will draw nigh to you. Cleanse your hands, ye sinners; and purify your hearts, ye double minded.

Be afflicted, and mourn, and weep: let your laughter be turned to mourning, and your joy to heaviness.

Humble yourselves in the sight of the Lord, and he shall lift you up.

James 4:7-10

Grace and peace be multiplied unto you through the knowledge of God, and of Jesus our Lord,

According as his divine power hath given unto us *all* things that pertain unto life and godliness, through the knowledge of him that hath called us to glory and virtue:

Whereby are given unto us exceeding great and precious promises: that by these ye might be partakers of the divine nature, having escaped the corruption that is in the world through lust.

And beside this, giving *all diligence*, add to your faith virtue; and to virtue knowledge;

And to knowledge temperance; and to temperance patience; and to patience godliness;

And to godliness brotherly kindness; and to brotherly kindness charity [love].

For if these things be in you, and abound, they make you that ye shall neither be barren nor unfruitful in the knowledge of our Lord Jesus Christ.

But he that lacketh these things is blind, and cannot see afar off, and hath forgotten that he was purged from his old sins.

Wherefore the rather, brethren, *give diligence* to make your calling and election sure: for *if* ye do these things, ye shall *never* fall:

For so an entrance shall be ministered unto you abundantly into the everlasting kingdom of our Lord and Saviour Jesus Christ.

2 Peter 1:2-11 (italics added for emphasis)

SOME BASIC TRUTHS FROM THE BIBLE
...

- God is Three persons, yet one God, revealed as the Father, the Son and the Holy Spirit. They are "personages" of Spirit Who are the same in substance, but distinct in subsistence.

- Jesus is God, the second person of the triune Godhead. He is spoken of as God the Son, as well as the Son of God.

- Jesus was born of the Virgin Mary.

- The baptism in the Holy Spirit. Speaking in tongues is the first sign of the baptism.

- Every believer should be water baptized in obedience to Jesus' command to His disciples. It is an outward sign of an inward grace.

- Salvation is "by grace, through faith," and is available to whosoever will choose to accept the free gift of God.

- The Bible is the infallible Word of God.

- There is a literal heaven, a literal hell and a literal lake of fire. Those who accept Jesus by faith, acknowledging His lordship and His resurrection, will spend eternity in heaven with the Lord. Those who reject Jesus will spend eternity separated from God in hell.

- Satan (the devil) is a literal being.

- Jesus is coming back to earth soon, just as He promised He would!

- Regular church attendance is commanded in the Bible. (See Hebrews 10:24,25.)

So you now have begun your eternal relationship with God by accepting Jesus as your Lord. In a very real sense, you have been taken to that "new country" we asked you earlier to only imagine. You will determine how quickly you learn about how things work in this new place. Be diligent and consistent at reading the Bible. It is your manual for living and for receiving the abundant life Jesus came to give you. It will take time and *diligent* effort on your part to grow in your relationship with God.

God loves you very much, and so do we. It is our hope that you will grow in the grace of our Lord Jesus as you continue in His Word and fellowship at church. Please consider making (your church's name) your church home. We would like very much to be a part of your becoming a disciple of Jesus.

About the Author

Rodney Lynch received Jesus in 1975. He attended Rhema Bible Training Center in 1985-86. He worked with Willie George Ministries from 1985 until 1990 when he became a staff member at Church on the Move in Tulsa, Oklahoma.

At Church on the Move, Rodney served as an associate minister for more than two years and was in charge of altar working, visitation and other areas of ministry. He is best known for his character portrayals on video presentations like "The Gospel Bill Show," "Fire By Nite" and other WGM productions.

He has been married for more than twenty years and has two children.

Rodney Lynch is available for meetings of youths and adults at your church. To contact him, write:

Rodney Lynch
P. O. Box 3315
Broken Arrow, OK 74013-3315

Please include your prayer requests and comments when you write.

Copies of this book are available
from your local bookstore.

Harrison House

Tulsa, Oklahoma 74153

In Canada contact:
Word Alive
P. O. Box 670
Niverville, Manitoba
CANADA R0A 1E0

The Harrison House Vision

Proclaiming the truth and the power
Of the Gospel of Jesus Christ
With excellence;

Challenging Christians to
Live victoriously,
Grow spiritually,
Know God intimately.